Gifford Pinchot

PRIVATE AND PUBLIC FORESTER

THIS BOOK IS THE
1968 AWARD WINNER
OF THE
AGRICULTURAL HISTORY SOCIETY

Gifford Pinchot

PRIVATE AND PUBLIC FORESTER

Harold T. Pinkett

UNIVERSITY OF ILLINOIS PRESS

Urbana, Chicago, London

© 1970 by the Board of Trustees of the University of Illinois.
Manufactured in the United States of America.
Library of Congress Catalog Card No. 74–76830.
252   00080   3

To LUCILLE

Preface

I WAS INTRODUCED to the forestry career of Gifford Pinchot many years ago, after I had been asked to prepare a descriptive inventory of records of the Forest Service, U.S. Department of Agriculture, in the National Archives. This inventory, my first major project in archival work, was written under the general direction of Theodore R. Schellenberg, then Chief of the Division of Agriculture Department Archives and later an Assistant Archivist of the National Archives and Records Service. Prior to that time I had read, of course, the usual history textbook references to Pinchot as a friend of Theodore Roosevelt, an apostle of conservation, and a protagonist in a famous controversy after the election of President William H. Taft.

My analysis of the records of the Forest Service combined with study of the rise and growth of this agency soon revealed to me Pinchot's towering stature in the history of American forestry and stimulated interest in research concerning basic motives, methods, and results of his work as a forester. Further interest in this direction was aroused by the publication of Pinchot's book, *Breaking New Ground*, which was called his "personal story" of the American forestry and conservation movements. Later study of varied aspects of government assistance in the protection and development of natural resources at The American University, Washington, D.C., and research in agricultural history at the National Archives gave additional impetus to the study of one whose leadership in resource conservation and management was continually conspicuous.

This research concerning Pinchot's forestry career involved extensive use of records of the Forest Service in the National Archives and the personal papers of Pinchot in the Manuscript Division, Library of Congress. The value of these and other primary sources is described in a bibliographical statement in this book. Published remarks of the forester and his associates and reports of government forest agencies that he headed provided important insights into many facets of his work.

Parts of Chapters IV and V are based upon information presented in the *North Carolina Historical Review* for July 1957 and in *New York History* for January 1958, for which permission to reprint was given by the State of North Carolina Department of Archives and History, and The New York State Historical Association, Cooperstown, N.Y., respectively. Harcourt, Brace and World, Inc., gave permission for the reprinting of several quotations from *Breaking New Ground*. Doubleday & Company, Inc., granted permission to quote from *Forests and Men*, by William B. Greeley. Photographs were obtained from the Forest Service with the generous cooperation of Leland J. Prater and Bluford W. Muir of the agency's photographic branch.

Important advice on several aspects of the study was given by the late Everett E. Edwards, chief agricultural historian of the U.S. Department of Agriculture; his successor, Wayne D. Rasmussen; Arthur E. Ekirch and Ernst Posner, former professors of history at The American University; and Elwood Maunder, Executive Director, Forest History Society. Miss Rachel Anderson, Assistant Editor, University of Illinois Press, carefully read the manuscript and gave many helpful suggestions to improve clarity and narration. These persons, of course, are not responsible for any errors that may appear in the book. Publication of the study had been made possible by a book award given by the Agricultural History Society in cooperation with the University of Illinois Press.

During all phases of research and writing for this book and in other scholarly endeavors the encouragement of my wife, Lucille C. Pinkett, has been an abiding inspiration. My indebtedness to her cannot be adequately expressed here but is affectionately acknowledged.

HAROLD T. PINKETT

Contents

Illustrations

Gifford Pinchot

PRIVATE AND PUBLIC FORESTER

I

Introduction

I HAVE . . . BEEN a Governor every now and then, but I am a forester all the time."[1] In these words Gifford Pinchot wished to emphasize what he considered the most vibrant interest of his varied career. He deliberately chose to place his work in forestry above his important role in state and national politics for more than a quarter-century. He stated a preference to be known as a forester rather than as a governor of an historic state or rather indeed as a close friend and adviser of one president of the United States and a powerful critic of several others.

But Pinchot was not just an ordinary forester. He was the first professionally trained American forester and the chief agent in the introduction of scientific forestry into the private and public woodlands of the United States. Out of his great interest in the preservation and development of forest resources grew his lifelong concern for the conservation of all natural resources. He came to be recognized as America's foremost apostle of conservation as well as its pioneer advocate of forestry. His deep, abiding interest in forestry was appropriately honored in 1949, when on June 15 a great national forest area along the Columbia River in Washington was renamed by presidential proclamation the Gifford Pinchot National Forest. The dedicatory ceremony took place in October. This area, formerly known as the Columbia National

---

[1] Gifford Pinchot, *Breaking New Ground* (New York, 1947), p. 137. This work will be cited hereafter as *Breaking New Ground*.

Forest, encompassing, 1,407,791 acres of majestic Douglas fir and yellow pine, grassy meadows, clear streams, and snow-clad peaks is a fitting tribute to the memory of a great friend of American forests. As the famous forester doubtless would have wished it, all memorial plaques and tablets in this forest refer only to his interest in forestry and conservation.

This study seeks to describe and appraise Pinchot's work in introducing scientific forest management on private and public timberlands of the United States and in reshaping forest policy and programs in Pennsylvania. Some facets of this work such as his role as a private forester in North Carolina and New York and as a promoter of forest research and training have not been treated in any considerable detail in politically oriented biographies of Pinchot and ideological studies of the early conservation movement.[2] Even the famous forester's own "personal story of how Forestry and Conservation came to America" (*Breaking New Ground*) deals only briefly with several aspects of his work that significantly affected the rise of American forestry.[3] Moreover, this story leaves room for further historical treatment since it was proudly written by one who played a great but controversial part in it and who presented it as an account not "decorated and delayed by references to [documentary] authorities" and one to be taken or left by readers largely on the author's "say-so." Other facets of Pinchot's forestry career such as his productive efforts in the movement for eastern national forests, strong criticism of Pennsylvania's state forest work, and ardent activity for the "restoration of Penn's Woods" have heretofore received hardly any historical treatment.

---

[2] M. Nelson McGeary's biography, *Gifford Pinchot, Forester-Politician* (Princeton, 1960) mentions outstanding experiences in Pinchot's forestry career but tends to describe in detail only those of great political significance. It does not deal with most of his work as a private forester and does not give any attention to his contribution to forest research and the movement for eastern national forests. Martin L. Fausold's work, *Gifford Pinchot, Bull Moose Progressive* (Syracuse, 1961) is a study of the political activities and ideas of Pinchot as a leader in the Progressive Party. The following perceptive studies of the conservation movement inevitably neglect or treat very briefly many of Pinchot's specialized and nonpolitical interests as a forester: Samuel P. Hays, *Conservation and the Gospel of Efficiency: The Progressive Conservation Movement, 1890–1920* (Cambridge, 1959); Elmo R. Richardson, *The Politics of Conservation, Crusades and Controversies, 1897–1913* (Berkeley and Los Angeles, 1962); and J. Leonard Bates, "Fulfilling American Democracy: The Conservation Movement, 1907 to 1921," *Mississippi Valley Historical Review,* XLIV (June 1957), 29–57.

[3] Pinchot's autobiography, *Breaking New Ground,* is limited to treatment of his experiences to 1910 and hence presents no information concerning his public forest work in Pennsylvania beginning in 1918.

The study begins with a history of the ideas and events that were conducive to the rise of efforts for forest protection in the United States and then shows how these efforts helped to produce the forestry movement in which Pinchot was to become the foremost leader. This is followed by an account and appraisal of his pioneering activities as a private forester and discussion of the evolution of the Forest Service, which under his direction spearheaded an historic effort for the conservation of forest and related natural resources. Later the several facets of Pinchot's role as the federal government's chief forester are delineated and assessed in relation to their contribution to American forestry and natural resource policy. Similarly treated in this context is his campaign for improved forest management in Pennsylvania. Throughout the study attention is focused on Pinchot's ideas and techniques as America's most innovative and influential forester.

That Gifford Pinchot was a man of action will be readily apparent in the chapters which follow. Thus, while attention is directed to one project or event in a multifaceted career, the reader must continually keep in mind that Pinchot, with his personal dynamism and commitment, was seldom if ever engaged in only one enterprise at a time; rather, under his shepherding or prodding guidance the whole issue of forestry was being, as it were, simultaneously developed and enlarged in many directions.

II

Genesis of American Forest Protection

THE IDEA THAT America was a land of inexhaustible natural wealth was one of the earliest and most persistent notions in the country's history. The reasons for the endurance of this impression are not difficult to find. To early American settlers the new continent was a cornucopia of every possible natural resource. The original forests of the United States contained timber in quantity and variety far beyond that of any other area of similar size in the world. Covering not less than 850,000,000 acres, these great forests contained some of the best stands of pine, oak, poplar, spruce, cedar, and fir ever recorded by history or geology. The soil was so rich and abundant in many places that only a small part of it was cultivated. The country was so vast that it did not seem possible that there could ever be a shortage of land. As time passed, Americans discovered greater and greater resources. They came into possession of fabulously rich deposits of gold, silver, and iron ores. They found vast anthracite, bituminous, and lignite coal lands and oil and gas fields scattered from the Appalachians to the Pacific coast. They discovered river systems which in extent, distribution, and ease of use were superior to those of any other country.[1]

---

[1] 60th Congress, 2d Sess., Senate Doc. No. 676, *Report of the National Conservation Commission*, I, 52–53, 75, 97–105; 60th Congress, 1st Sess., Senate Doc. No. 325, *Preliminary Report of the Inland Waterways Commission*, p. 1.

6

It is not surprising, therefore, that the legend of unlimited natural wealth in America developed. The legend began with Columbus when in a prospectus on the new world he wrote about "fields very green and full of an infinity of fruits" and regions where gold was "found among the roots of trees, along the banks and among the rocks and stones left by torrents."[2] Later, American explorers, travelers, and speculators helped to perpetuate the idea of inexhaustibility. In 1721 tracing the path of Marquette and La Salle, Pierre Charlevoix exclaimed, "We are in the midst of the greatest forests in the world. . . . They are as old as the world itself. . . . There is nothing perhaps in nature comparable to them."[3] Glowing accounts of the rich resources of the West came from the expeditions of George Vancouver, Lewis and Clark, Stephen H. Long, and many others. A typical impression was voiced by a traveler in 1826: "There are no richer soils on the globe than the alluvial land along the Ohio, the Mississippi, and other rivers of the West. 'The American Bottom,' so called in the State of Illinois, is of inexhaustible fertility."[4] To Washington Irving the Prairies in 1832 seemed to contain regions which answered literally to the description of the land of promise, since the rich pasturage was "calculated to sustain herds of cattle as countless as the sands upon the seashore."[5]

Thus generation after generation Americans had been told that their natural resources were inexhaustible and because of the unprecedented abundance of these resources they had come to believe that such was true. But of greater consequence was the fact that they used the resources as though they truly were inexhaustible. By the close of the nineteenth century a great drain had been made on this great natural wealth. Much of the depletion had come in the sacred name of national development. The pioneer had cleared away much of the American primeval forest as an obstacle to the use of land. "He waged a hand-to-hand war upon it," declared Frederick Jackson Turner, "cutting and burning a little space to let in the light upon a dozen acres of hard-won soil and year after year expanding the clearing into new woodlands against the stubborn resistance of primeval trunks and matted roots."[6]

---

[2] Cited from Russell Lord, *Behold Our Land* (Boston, 1938), p. 77.
[3] Pierre Charlevoix, Letters, pp. 92, 306. Cited from Jenks Cameron, *Development of Government Forest Control in the United States* (Baltimore, 1928), p. 5.
[4] Soil Erosion History Data, excerpt from *The Berks and Schuylkill Journal*, Reading, Pa., July 15, 1826, Record Group 114 Records of the Soil Conservation Service, National Archives.
[5] Washington Irving, *A Tour of the Prairies* (New York, 1833), p. 31.
[6] Frederick J. Turner, *The Frontier in American History* (New York, 1920), p. 270.

The lumber companies which came later, though bent on selling timber, had found it profitable to take only the best of the forests and destroy the remainder. With new fields of virgin land always lying just beyond them, most early farmers had seen no need to conserve the fertile soil. Commercial groups had competed, often unscrupulously, with home makers for possession of the rich resources of the public domain and had used them with little regard for the needs of future generations. The march of these events by 1890 led Gifford Pinchot to observe,

> The Nation was obsessed . . . by a fury of development. The American Colossus was fiercely intent on appropriating and exploiting the riches of the richest of all continents — grasping with both hands, reaping where he had not sown, wasting what he thought would last forever.[7]

The ruthless exploitation of natural resources was first most obvious and alarming in the continuing devastation of the nation's forests. Concern about this trend produced a forest preservation movement, out of which grew efforts for scientific management of forests and other natural resources. Although Gifford Pinchot was the most effective and successful leader of these endeavors, other Americans before him had recognized in varying degrees the need for forest protection. As early as 1817 Congress had feared the possibility of a general shortage of naval ship-construction timber (mainly live oak) and had reserved certain public lands of the Southeast as a source of timber for naval purposes. Later it provided for the planting of trees and some measures designed to prevent theft and destruction on public timberlands. Unfortunately, this early Federal interest in forest conservation lapsed after the substitution of iron and steel for oak in naval vessels.[8]

Interest in forest preservation became more widespread during the third quarter of the nineteenth century, and appeals were voiced for some form of public action to halt the destructive practices. In 1864 George P. Marsh, an American diplomat and extensive traveler, in a provocative geographical work had warned: "It is certain that a desolation like that which has overwhelmed many once beautiful and fertile regions of Europe, awaits an important part of the territory of the United States, unless prompt measures are taken to check the action of

---

[7] *Breaking New Ground*, p. 23.

[8] Arthur P. Chew, *The Response of Government to Agriculture* (Washington, 1937), p. 42. (U.S.D.A.)

destructive causes already in operation."[9] Two years later the United States Commissioner of Agriculture in his annual report published a similar warning written by the Reverend Mr. Frederick Starr of St. Louis, Missouri.[10] That the words of Marsh, Starr, and a few others did not go entirely unheeded was evident when several states, notably in the prairie region, attempted to remedy the situation by encouraging forest planting through tax exemptions and bounties. Thus began a "tree planting" movement, from which in 1872 emerged the popular "Arbor Day" idea from Nebraska. Furthermore, the federal government in 1873 enacted the "Timber-Culture Law," which aimed to encourage forestation by requiring the planting and successful growing of a certain number of trees as the consideration of a deed to a quarter-section of the public domain. In the same year a committee of the American Association for the Advancement of Science memorialized Congress for the appointment of a Federal Commissioner to conduct forest investigations. Congress responded three years later by appropriating $2,000 for a study of forest conditions in the United States by an official to be appointed by the Commissioner of Agriculture. Dr. Franklin B. Hough, the spearhead of this action by the Association, was appointed to conduct the investigations. In this modest way the Federal Government began forestry work.[11]

This step was indeed modest as far as the forest preservation movement was concerned, for it was no major departure from past public policy. Since it made no provision for better management of the timbered areas of the public domain, these areas remained under the control of the Interior Department's General Land Office whose diligence and facilities for forest preservation were doubtful, to say the least. Especially ironical was the situation created where one department, Agriculture, was placed in charge of forestry without forests, while another, Interior, remained in charge of forests without forestry. It is not surprising that later, as the first professionally trained American forester, Pinchot would regard this situation as intolerable.

Despite criticisms of its General Land Office, the Department of the Interior through Carl Schurz, one of its greatest secretaries, did respond constructively to the demand for forest preservation. Primarily as a

---

[9] George P. Marsh, *Man and Nature* (New York, 1864), p. 233. This work was better known under the title, *The Earth as Modified by Human Action*, as published ten years later.

[10] U.S. Department of Agriculture, *Report of the Commissioner of Agriculture for the Year 1866* (Washington, 1866), pp. 210–234.

[11] Darrell H. Smith, *The Forest Service* (Washington, 1930), pp. 4–6.

result of his energies, a policy of federal reservation and administration of the public timberlands was set up as an objective.[12] As Secretary of the Interior, he launched a vigorous offensive against timber depredations on the public domain. As a further preventive measure, he recommended in 1877 that all timberlands still belonging to the United States should be withdrawn from the operation of the pre-emption and homestead laws, a sufficient number of government agents should be provided to prevent the stealing of timber, and criminal as well as civil action should be instituted against the depredators.[13] For the 1870's these were audacious recommendations. It was no surprise that they failed to receive legislative sanction at that time. Reminiscing on this effort, Schurz later stated: "What I did with regard to the public forests was simply to arrest devastation, in which I partially succeeded, and for which I was lustily denounced, and to strive from year to year to obtain from Congress legislation for the protection of the forests, in which I largely failed."[14]

Schurz' agitating, however, was not in vain. His bold advocacy of protection of the public timberlands became a rallying point for various groups interested in forest preservation. At the same time these groups were increasingly impressed by the reported success of European forest protection, especially with regard to communal forests. They succeeded in getting some states to act well in advance of the Federal Government. Legislators in Massachusetts, for example, were persuaded in 1882 to enact a law which authorized the condemnation of land for community forest purposes and established a board of forestry.[15] During the 1880's forestry boards or commissions were inaugurated in other states and there emerged private organizations devoted to forestry. The American Forestry Association of today grew out of the American Forestry Congress which was organized in Cincinnati, Ohio, in April 1882. This congress was the first extensive gathering of American advocates of forest preservation.[16] It was also notable in that it brought into prominence Dr. Bernhard E. Fernow, who was to be-

---

[12] Herbert A. Smith, "The Early Forestry Movement in the United States," *Agricultural History*, XII (October 1938), 341.

[13] U.S. Department of the Interior, *Report of the Secretary, 1877* (Washington, 1878), p. 19.

[14] Frederic Bancroft (ed.) *Speeches, Correspondence, and Political Papers of Carl Schurz* (New York, 1913), VI, 38–39.

[15] J. P. Kinney, *The Development of Forest Law in America* (New York, 1917), p. 210.

[16] Cameron, *Development of Governmental Forest Control in the United States*, p. 196.

come, in 1886, the first trained forester to direct governmental forest work in the United States. Fernow, German-born and trained at the Forest Academy of Münden, Prussia, talked to the congress on the development of forest policy in Germany where, he stated, the necessity for forest care and reforestation was recognized as early as Charlemagne's time. (On this score, the American "Arbor Day" could be considered reminiscent of long-established European forest policies.[17]) Another voice of European experience was also heard. In a letter of greetings to the Congress, Richard von Steuben, Royal Chief Forester of the German Empire, declared:

> There can be no doubt that every country requires a certain quantity of well stocked woods, not only to supply the demands for building material and fuel, but more especially to secure suitable meteorological conditions, to preserve the fertility of the soil, and out of sanitary considerations. . . . In Germany, and especially in my more narrowly bounded fatherland, Prussia, it is regarded as of the greatest importance, not only to preserve the forests already there, but to extend them as much as possible.[18]

In general, the American Forestry Congress of 1882 called attention to what other nations had done and were doing to combat forest destruction, and prompted recommendations for the initiation of public measures for reforestation and the superintendence and preservation of American forests that had so far escaped destruction.

It should be pointed out, however, that basically the forest preservation movement furthered by the American Forestry Congress and certain writers centered upon the idea of tree planting, which in the vocabulary of the period was called "tree culture," "forest culture," and "timber culture." This congress and the writings of George P. Marsh, Franklin B. Hough, Bernhard E. Fernow, and others did help to acquaint Americans with the current scientific thought in Europe concerning forest influences and the dangers arising from forest destruction. While these factors stimulated some remedial action, they also tended to give an exaggerated idea of the importance of artificial reforestation and thereby led to a false start for American forestry, with tree planting as its principal concern. Later Pinchot and other trained foresters had to convince Americans "that the practice of forestry is primarily a matter of continuous management of existing forests, with dependence chiefly

---

[17] The (Cincinnati) *Enquirer*, April 27, 1882.
[18] The Cincinnati *Commercial*, April 26, 1882.

on natural reproduction, not tree planting, for replacement of the stand." [19] The acceptance of this concept in America was to open the way for the inauguration of a broad program for forest management.

Meanwhile advancement of American forest protection, though not management, was aided by a movement for the preservation of historic and scenic areas — the movement out of which was to evolve the national park system. Efforts toward this end were made as early as 1850, when Secretary of the Interior Alexander Stuart "suggested that 'Mount Vernon whose soil was once tilled by the hands and is now consecrated by the dust of the Father of his Country, should properly belong to the Nation,' and that it should become a model farm to illustrate the progress of agriculture, to which George Washington was devoted." [20] Twenty years later a group of Montanans explored the Yellowstone area in Montana, Wyoming, and Idaho, and were so impressed by the area's numerous geysers, remarkable waterfalls, and deep canyons that they recommended its preservation as a great national park. Resulting interest and attention led to a Congressional act which created Yellowstone National Park in March 1872. This legislation stipulated that the Secretary of the Interior should make regulations to "provide for the preservation, from injury or spoilation, of all timber, mineral deposits, natural curiosities, or wonders, within the park, and their retention in their natural condition." [21] By the end of the nineteenth century, the concern for preservation of historic and scenic woodland areas had led to the establishment of several other parks, including Yosemite, Sequoia, General Grant, and Mount Ranier National Parks.

During this same period, bills providing for some form of Federal forest reservation were being introduced in Congress in increasing number with increasing national support. The opposition of antagonistic Western interests, however, was too formidable to be overcome until 1891, when through Congress there crept virtually unnoticed a briefly worded amendment authorizing the President to establish forest reserves from the public domain.[22] Under this enactment, in the autumn of 1891, President Benjamin Harrison proclaimed the creation of the Yellowstone National Park Timber Land Reserve in Wyoming and the White River Plateau Timber Land Reserve in Colorado, with a combined area of 2,437,120 acres. During the next two years Presidents Har-

---

[19] Herbert A. Smith, p. 328.
[20] Cited from U.S. Department of the Interior, A Century of Conservation (Washington, 1950), Conservation Bulletin 39, p. 10.
[21] 17 Stat. L., 32 (March 1, 1872).
[22] 26 Stat. L., 1095 (March 3, 1891).

rison and Grover Cleveland set aside as forest reserves more than 17,500,000 acres exclusive of some 3,000 acres which lay within the borders of Yellowstone, Yosemite, Sequoia, and General Grant National Parks.[23] These reserves were the seeds from which grew the national forests of the United States.

With the act of 1891 the forest preservation movement took a step forward, but it was only a step. It gave the newly created forest reserves no form of management and left them without protection except that which the General Land Office could give with its small and untrained force. Moreover, legally at least, it withdrew areas of considerable natural resources from every form of use by the people of the West or by the Federal Government. The resulting anti-forestry sentiment among many groups lingered long after the forests had been thrown open for various uses.

Several attempts, notably by Representative Thomas C. McRae of Arkansas and Senator Algernon S. Paddock of Nebraska, were made to remedy the deficiencies of the forest law of 1891. Their efforts were supported by Secretary of the Interior Hoke Smith. After these efforts had failed, the American Forestry Association in 1896 asked the Secretary to request the National Academy of Sciences, the legally constituted adviser of the Government in scientific matters, to investigate the entire forestry question and report "upon the inauguration of a rational forest policy for the forested lands of the United States."[24] Dr. Wolcott Gibbs, president of the Academy, responded favorably on its behalf to Secretary Smith's request. With great insight he declared:

> No subject upon which the Academy has been asked before by the Government for advice compares with it in scope, and it is the opinion of thoughtful men that no other economic problem confronting the Government of the United States equals in importance that offered by the present condition and future fate of the forests of western North America.[25]

Gibbs named a National Forest Commission of seven men. Charles S. Sargent, Professor of Arboriculture in Harvard University and Director of the Harvard Botanic Garden and the Arnold Arboretum, was selected as Chairman. Sargent was already an influential figure in the American

---

[23] Cameron, p. 205.

[24] 55th Congress, 1st Sess., Senate Doc. No. 105, *Report of the Committee Appointed by the National Academy of Sciences Upon the Inauguration of a Forest Policy for the Forested Lands of the United States*, p. 7.

[25] Cited from *Breaking New Ground*, p. 90.

forest preservation movement largely as a result of his chairmanship of the New York State Forest Commission, his publication of the journal *Garden and Forest*, and his famous volume titled *American Forest Trees*, which had been published in the Tenth Census. The Commission also included Henry L. Abbot, an Army engineer and authority on the physics and hydraulics of streams; Alexander Agassiz, Curator of the Harvard Museum of Comparative Zoology; William H. Brewer, Professor of Agriculture in Yale's Sheffield Scientific School; Wolcott Gibbs, member ex officio, a noted chemist and physicist; and Arnold Hague, a geologist in the United States Geological Survey.

Last, but certainly not least, on the Commission and the only one who was not a member of the National Academy was Gifford Pinchot. His distinction lay in the fact that he was the only member of the Commission possessing scientific forestry training and experience. Indeed he was then the only American-born professional forester. Thus, in a situation requiring the best available knowledge of American forests and the best advice on their preservation, Pinchot was eminently qualified to render outstanding service. In a sense he could be expected to be one, perhaps the only one, who knew the road on which the country must march out of the forest wilderness of neglect and destruction. Yet here was a young man of thirty-one on a national commission of distinguished scientists whose average age was more than twice his own. Most Americans, who in 1896 could not even correctly spell or pronounce Pinchot's name, naturally wondered how he had come into such national prominence. They were not to forget his name, because from that time onward through half a century it was to be continually associated with all efforts to protect and manage forests and the related natural wealth of America.

III

Education of America's First Forester

To SOME OF HIS CRITICS who called him a mere theorist and dreamer and to others who even hinted that his ideas were un-American, Gifford Pinchot liked to say that he was born a Connecticut Yankee. And so he was, though his fame and fortune were to be more intimately associated with another state. He was born at Simsbury, Connecticut, on August 11, 1865. He could boast further of the democratic tradition of his family, for his grandfather, Cyril Constantine Désiré Pinchot, a Huguenot, had come to America in 1815 in search of political and religious freedom. Gifford was the eldest son of James W. Pinchot, a wealthy manufacturer in New York and Pennsylvania. His mother, Mary (Eno) Pinchot, was a direct descendant of William Phelps, who was one of the founders of Windsor, Connecticut, and the progenitor of a family prominent during the American colonial and revolutionary periods. Gifford was named after Sanford Gifford, the famous American landscape painter, one of a coterie of artists and literary men with whom his father mingled.[1]

Young Pinchot received most of his earliest formal education in private schools in Paris and New York City, where his parents lived for several years. He later attended historic Phillips Exeter Academy in

---

[1] A good account of Pinchot's family background and early life appears in McGeary, *Gifford Pinchot, Forester-Politician* (Princeton, 1960), pp. 3–28.

New Hampshire and entered Yale University in 1885. In the summer just before he went to Yale, his father asked the strange question: "How would you like to be a forester?"[2] Gifford, like the average American of the time, had no conception of what it meant to be a forester in the modern sense. He wondered what a modern forester did. He assumed that such a person no longer wore a green cap and a leather jerkin and shot cloth-yard arrows at deer in royal forests. But he knew little else except that a forester worked in and with the woods and that he himself through camping and hunting had come to love the woods. The elder Pinchot, however, had seen foresters and their work in France and elsewhere in Europe. In his reading of French history he had become a great admirer of Colbert, Louis XIV's great finance minister, and Bernard Palissy, naturalist and philosopher, both of whom had emphasized the fundamental relation between forests and national welfare. He was familiar with the protests against forest destruction that were being made by a few of his American contemporaries, he had come to believe that American forests would be saved not by mere protests, but rather by the practice of scientific forestry. Impressed deeply by his father's thinking and encouragement and prompted by his own love for the woods, young Pinchot decided that forestry would be his profession.

In 1885 no systematic program of study in forestry was available at Yale, or indeed at any American university. However, there were related courses in meteorology, botany, geology, and astronomy. Pinchot took such courses and hoped that he was at least headed in the right direction. He read every book on forestry that he could find in the Yale Library, thus learning something of forest conditions from Marsh's provocative work, *The Earth as Modified by Human Action*, Sargent's comprehensive study of American forests, and a book entitled *Studies in Forest Economy* written by a French forester, Jules Clavé. Perhaps his greatest source of knowledge about forests and American conditions in general derived from discussions with Yale Professor William H. Brewer. Having explored much of the West and published a study of American forest distribution in Walker's *Statistical Atlas of the Ninth Census*, Brewer impressed Pinchot as being a "wise and kindly compendium of universal information" ever "ready to lecture, or give a whole course of lectures, at a moment's notice" on any subject including forests.[3]

---

[2] *Breaking New Ground*, p. 1.
[3] *Breaking New Ground*, p. 3–4.

During his senior year he went to Washington to confer with government officials regarding his plan to be a forester. No encouragement was given by these men. George B. Loring, who had recently retired as Commissioner of Agriculture, could see little chance for an American to find work as a forester. Bernhard E. Fernow, the German forester, then Chief of the Forestry Division of the Department of Agriculture, advised Pinchot against pursuing forestry as a profession and suggested that he might rather study it with a view to preparing for work in landscape gardening, nursery business, or botany. Professor Sargent at Harvard concurred. At the same time Gifford's grandfather, Amos R. Eno, one of the wealthiest men in New York City, urged him to think less of the forest and more of a fortune. Notwithstanding, his father continued to encourage him in his plan. Qualified support was also forthcoming from Dr. Joseph T. Rothrock, already a leading advocate of forest protection in Pennsylvania and later to be acclaimed as the State's father of forest conservation. To the Yale student Dr. Rothrock admitted that he hardly knew what advice to offer, but he expressed a conviction that there would be "a limited number of openings for trained foresters from General and State governments and from timber owning companies" for which trained men were not then available.[4]

His four years at Yale passed quickly and happily. When he was not studying about forests, he found time to act as a class deacon, play football, write for the *Yale Literary Magazine*, and work in the YMCA. Graduation day came in June 1889. After Mark Twain and other commencement speakers had finished, orations by members of the graduating class were in order. Pinchot, who had carefully prepared a speech on some nonforestry subject, was suddenly struck with the desire to say something about forests. Thus he discarded his prepared speech and made to the Yale gathering his first public profession of faith in the importance of forestry to the United States — a faith that was to remain undimmed and unshaken through a long, varied, and stormy public career.

He had plenty of faith in forestry but still little real knowledge of it. Thus in the summer of 1889 he seized an opportunity to learn more by attending the World Exposition in Paris. Here he viewed a special exhibit on waters and forests and obtained some scientific treatises on forestry. More important on this European trip, however, was his

---

[4] Joseph T. Rothrock to Pinchot, March 12, 1888, Gifford Pinchot Papers, Library of Congress, Washington, D.C. (The Pinchot Papers are cited hereafter as GPP.)

chance to meet two of the world's greatest foresters, Sir William Schlich and Sir Dietrich Brandis. Schlich, a former Inspector General of Forests to the Government of India, cordially received Pinchot at the British Forest School at Cooper's Hill, which he then directed for the training of foresters for India; he gave him an autographed copy of his *Manual of Forestry*, and urged him to work for the creation of national forests in the United States. Expressing regret that regulations did not permit the admission of Pinchot to his school, Schlich encouraged the young American to pursue the study of forestry and recommended his subsequent meeting with Brandis in Germany. Brandis, who had inaugurated forest management in the government forests of British India, was immediately impressed by Pinchot's earnestness and readily consented to show him the way to scientific forestry.[5] Reminiscing on his own youthful, pioneering endeavors in India beginning in 1856, this famous forester may well have seen in his young visitor the instrument for establishing forestry in America.

On the recommendation of Brandis, French foresters, and possibly U.S. Forestry Division Chief Fernow, Pinchot in November 1889 became a student at the widely recognized French Forest School in Nancy.[6] Here he studied silviculture, the art of producing and caring for forests; economic matters such as forest capital, rent, interest, and sustained yield; and forest law based upon the Code Napoléon. He acquired much useful information about forestry in the school's lecture rooms, but he learned much more from his walks and observations in the forests of Haye and Vandoeuvres north of Nancy near Verdun. These forests, managed by professional foresters, were grown, harvested, and reproduced like a crop, and protected from fire and harmful cutting to a degree unknown in America.

In the spring of 1890, Brandis arranged for Pinchot to spend a month with Forstmeister Meister, an internationally famous Swiss forester who had charge of the ancient Sihlwald, a municipal forest of Zurich. This woodland, which Brandis regarded as the most instructive forest area in Europe, had been under systematic and profitable management before the discovery of America. Meister gave Pinchot every opportu-

---

[5] *Breaking New Ground*, p. 7.

[6] Pinchot in *Breaking New Ground* (pp. 7 ff.) credited only Brandis and French foresters with the recommendation to attend the French Forest School. Fernow, however, in a letter of May 31, 1895 to J. Rothschild, Editor of *Revue des Eaux et Forêts*, stated: "I invariably recommend to Americans, who wish to study forestry, the forestry school at Nancy, and it was I who sent Mr. Gifford Pinchot . . . to Nancy." Record Group 95, Records of the Forest Service, National Archives (cited hereafter as RG 95.)

nity to learn about the management of the Sihlwald, and, being not only a forester but also a political leader, writer, and newspaper publisher, he gave him some insights into the methods and importance of winning public opinion for a cause. Thus the education of Pinchot as publicist as well as forester was now under way.

After a trip of forest observation through the French Alps and the Vosges, Pinchot joined Brandis in the summer of 1890 for an excursion through some of the model forests of Germany and Switzerland where he met and talked with some of Europe's best foresters and saw many of its best managed timberlands. Most of these forest authorities urged him to study a year or two longer. But he had begun to feel that some European theories and methods of forestry did not conform to American needs and that consequently he did not need the full, long, and intensive training program taken by a prospective European forester. Moreover, a prediction from his father that conditions in America would soon be ripe for scientific forestry doubtless made him believe that he should begin to use the training that he had already obtained. Hence, in December 1890 he returned home. Many years later when he wrote *Breaking New Ground*, he expressed some regret for failure to continue his formal training to the point of a doctorate in forestry, and conceded that although he had "some acquaintance with forest management in action," he was in a general professional sense "no more than half-trained."[7]

In any event, his training was soon tested, for he was invited to present on December 30, 1890, a paper on "Government Forestry Abroad" at a joint session of the American Economic Association and the American Forestry Association in Washington, D.C. Here he met leaders of the forest preservation movement such as Rothrock of Pennsylvania, Warren Higley of New York, and Edward A. Bowers, former federal public lands inspector and later Assistant Commissioner of the General Land Office. He also saw Fernow who repeated an earlier offer of a position as his assistant in the Division of Forestry. Pinchot's paper at the meeting, admittedly "hastily prepared" mainly from published materials, sketched forest developments in Europe, Australia, India, South Africa, and Japan, but dealt mainly with Germany, France, and Switzerland where he felt forestry had reached greatest development and where he had been privileged to observe it.[8] The paper noted that in all of these places forest management could be said to rest on two axio-

---

[7] Pinchot to Brandis, August 21, 1893, GPP; *Breaking New Ground*, p. 30.
[8] Gifford Pinchot, "Government Forestry Abroad," *Publications of the American Economic Association*, VI (May 1891), 191–238.

matic facts, "first, that trees require many years to reach merchantable size; and secondly, that a forest crop cannot be taken every year from the same land." It therefore followed that a "far-seeing plan is necessary for the rational management of any forest" and that "forest property is safest under supervision of some imperishable guardian" such as the State.

In his discussion of German forest policy, Pinchot mentioned the prominent place given to the theory of the State's duty to preserve forests for their economic value both to present and future generations — a concept dominant in his crusading conservation speeches of later years. Although he valued knowledge of Germany's advanced and minute forest methods for comparative purposes, he warned against blind imitation of them in America where they might be inappropriate by reason of peculiarities of national character as well as climate, soil, forest, transportation, supply and demand, any many other factors. Understandably, he spoke favorably of the French government's program of forestry training at Nancy and praised its relatively high annual revenue from public forests, which, in his view, placed French forest management on a basis "very far removed from sentimentation and the philanthropic forest protection whose watchword is 'Hands off.'" Switzerland, however, with its republican traditions and flexible application of forestry principles to immediate situations, won Pinchot's warmest praise and evoked the suggestion that Swiss methods might well be a model for study by American advocates of forest reform. He concluded the paper with a strong indictment of the "calamitous results" of forest destruction in the United States and a ringing declaration prompted by experience of foreign governments: "The care of the forests is the duty of the nation."

Gifford Pinchot, consulting forester, resting near Partlow Lake in the Adirondacks. The picture was taken in March 1898 by his friend and colleague
Henry S. Graves, while the two foresters were conducting an experiment
in forestry on the woodland property of William C. Whitney.   (p. 37)

In the company of officials of the U.S. Department of Agriculture and Forest Service, June 15, 1949, President Truman presents to Dr. Gifford Bryce Pinchot, son of Gifford Pinchot, and grandson, Gifford, the pen with which the President signed the proclamation that changed the name of the Columbia National Forest, Washington, to the Gifford Pinchot National Forest, to "establish a living tribute to the good works of a public servant by naming a national forest in his honor." (p. 3)

IV

Trail Blazing in Southern Woodlands

WHEN HE RETURNED from his European studies in 1890, Pinchot found the United States still without a single acre of public or private timberland under systematic forest management. He had no success with Brandis' suggestion that his wealthy grandfather Eno be asked to buy a tract on which he might demonstrate forest management.[1] Nevertheless, an opportunity to make use of his training did come early, when he was hired by the firm of Phelps, Dodge and Company to make a preliminary examination of its white pine and hemlock lands in Pennsylvania and report on the possibilities of practicing forestry upon them. The lands were in Monroe County and also in familiar Pike County, where his forebears had lived near Milford since 1816. Pinchot's findings are not now available, but it may well have been, as he claimed, "the first practical report on the application of Forestry to a particular forest ever made in America."[2] Shortly after this experience he was invited to accompany Fernow on a trip to inspect an area of timberland in the Mississippi bottoms in eastern Arkansas. Here Pinchot had his first opportunity to learn something about the huge hardwood trees of the Mississippi Valley, work methods of tough Arkansas lumberjacks, and mores of an unfamiliar southern

---

[1] Pinchot to James W. Pinchot and Mary E. Pinchot, September 21, 1890, GPP.
[2] *Breaking New Ground*, p. 37.

region. He spent ten days in the Arkansas flatwoods and then traveled
with Fernow to Mobile, Alabama, to see Dr. Charles Mohr, prominent
botanist and forest protection advocate and an important agent of
Fernow's Division in the study of southern white pine trees. The Forestry Division chief left him with Dr. Mohr to assist in a survey of
mixed forests in northern Alabama. This southern trip was helpful in
broadening the young forester's knowledge of American forests, but
was not without unpleasantness, since it gave him an impression of
Fernow as an extremely domineering and vain individual that chilled
future relations between the two men.[3]

A few weeks later in the spring of 1891 Gifford was on another forest
inspection trip for Phelps, Dodge and Company which carried him to
the West Coast and Canada. To this eastern tenderfoot the trip was notable for its initial and kaleidoscopic panoramas of the still largely unde-
veloped western United States. Its primary purpose was an examination
of an unpromising arid forest tract in the Sulphur Spring Valley of
Arizona, then extensively infested with mesquite and sagebrush and
exposed to frequent trespass by Apache Indians. Upon completion of
this examination Pinchot headed north on an itinerary that unfolded
the serene splendor of the Grand Canyon, magnificent stands of
eucalyptus in the San Gabriel Valley of California, famed groves of
giant sequoias on the slopes of the Sierra Nevada, vast Douglas-fir saw-
mills in Oregon and Washington, and gigantic spruce in Vancouver's
Stanley Park. He was able to observe also some of the ugly marks on
the great western scene left by countless years of uncontrolled forest
fires and rampaging floods. When he returned home at the beginning
of summer he could take pride in the fact that within six months of
his return from Europe he had seen something of forests in thirty-one
American states and Canada (though largely only from the train) and
had actually examined them in nine states.

It was in February 1892 that Pinchot, the student and advocate of
forestry, became its first American-born practitioner. The scene of this
event was the estate acquired and developed by George W. Vanderbilt
at Biltmore in western North Carolina on the great continental table-
land between the Blue Ridge and Allegheny Mountains. Here Pinchot
arrived on February 21 to begin an urgent and unique experiment. A
contract with Vanderbilt provided an annual salary of $2,500, for which

---

[3] *Breaking New Ground*, p. 38; Pinchot's diary, February 3, and March 14, 1891,
GPP.

he had agreed to make a plan for the management of Biltmore Forest and to superintend the preparation of an exhibit of this forest for the World's Columbian Exposition to be held at Chicago the following year.[4] He had been selected for this job apparently on the recommendation of Frederick Law Olmsted, the famous landscape architect, who was Vanderbilt's principal adviser in the planning of the Biltmore Estate. The preparation of a management plan for an American forest in 1892 was an undertaking without any precedent and with little relevant information. Yet it was a project urgently needed to demonstrate the practicality of scientific forestry in the United States and to broaden the movement for the preservation of American forests. Fortunately, it was a task to which Pinchot could bring some unique training and valuable experience.

When Pinchot arrived at the Biltmore Estate, development of the property, which was to make it one of America's most luxurious country residences, had already begun. Under the architectural direction of Richard M. Hunt the massive limestone walls of the French Renaissance Biltmore House were rising as if to challenge the grandeur of nearby mountains. The estate, lying southeast of Asheville, stretched six miles along the banks of the French Broad River and covered more than 7,000 acres. Through its northeast corner ran the Swannanoa River toward its junction with the French Broad. Broken, hilly land alternated with broad alluvial bottoms of the rivers.

By 1892 much forest land around the site selected for Biltmore House was in process of consolidation into a large holding as a result of Vanderbilt's purchases from a number of small landholders. Compelled by economic necessity to exploit fully their scantily productive lands, these persons had resorted to destructive practices. They had cut most of the trees which could be used or sold as fuel, fence wood, or saw logs. Thus the best species had been removed and the inferior ones had remained to seed the ground and perpetuate their kind. Worse yet, in accordance with a long-established practice, the small landholders had burned the woods each year in the belief that better pasturage was thus obtained the following year. In this way much of the fertility of the soil had been destroyed. Young trees which grew up in many places had been cut back year after year for the grazing of cattle. The condition of a large part of the forest was "deplorable in the extreme," in Pinchot's eyes. The timber stands that had survived these destructive

---

[4] Agreement between Pinchot and Vanderbilt, January 25, 1892, GPP.

practices were dominated by various species of oak, shortleaf pine, and chestnut. Most of the stands were broken and irregular and varied greatly in size and age.[5]

Although he was given a free hand to inaugurate management of the Biltmore Estate's forest, subject only to Vanderbilt's control, Pinchot's work was affected inevitably by considerations of the general purpose of the estate as a country residence, with its gardens, farms, deer park, and roads. His management was, therefore, subject to checks in instances where silvicultural measures were considered to conflict with landscape, farming, recreational, or other estate purposes. Despite restrictions, the young forester began work at Biltmore with the hope and zeal of a missionary. His decision to undertake the work, he said, was largely influenced by the often expressed opinion of Sir Dietrich Brandis that forest management in the United States must begin through private enterprise, and his own feeling that the Chicago exposition would present a good opportunity to publicize the beginning of "practical forestry." [6] If forest management could be made profitable at Biltmore, it could be made so in almost any part of the Southern Appalachians. Indeed his hope led him to assert, "The more I know of the conditions the more thoroughly satisfied I am that if Biltmore forest is a success, I need not fear to undertake the management of any piece of forest land that I have seen in the United States." [7]

Compilation of detailed data concerning forest conditions on the estate was Pinchot's first step. This was facilitated by an extensive topographical survey of the property which had already been made. The survey had divided the estate into squares of 500 feet. The squares were used as units of description and pertinent silvicultural data were recorded in a card catalogue. Using this information Pinchot divided the forest area into ninety-two compartments, averaging about forty-two acres each and delimited by ridges, streams, hollows, or roads. For management purposes he grouped these compartments into three blocks, one situated west of the French Broad River and two east of it.[8]

The general purposes of the pioneering forestry work at Biltmore were to promote the profitable production of timber, provide a nearly constant annual yield, and improve the condition of the forest. The effort began with so-called "improvement cuttings" in parts of the forest

[5] Gifford Pinchot, *Biltmore Forest* (Chicago, 1893), pp. 10–14.
[6] Pinchot to Brandis, February 2, 1892, GPP.
[7] Pinchot to Brandis, March 5, 1892, GPP.
[8] Pinchot, *Biltmore Forest*, pp. 22 ff.

where old trees were sufficiently numerous and the younger ones sufficiently vigorous to enable profitable lumbering. In these cuttings Pinchot had to instruct his forest assistants and woods crews to fell timber in such a manner that the least harm would come to the future forest. This objective, emphasizing regard for future use as well as for immediate profit, was new in American lumbering. Demonstration and acceptance of the value of this new principle were critical for the successful introduction of scientific forestry into the United States and establishment of the concept that forest preservation in the 1890's was not necessarily incompatible with profitable use of forests.

Although Pinchot was convinced of the scientific propriety and educational value of careful timber cuttings, he was by no means certain that the timber thus produced could compete successfully with that provided by traditional lumbering methods. Early in his work he was disturbed by the doubtful outlook for immediate "money returns" from the forest. In his words, "There is so much good lumber in the mountains, it is comparatively so cheap and our own is so distinctly poor, that we shall certainly be unable to do more than supply a little inferior sawn lumber and some fire wood for the local market and engage in the wood-distilling industry." [9] Nor were his hopes raised any higher by the gloomy opinion of the federal government's chief forester: "If you can make forestry profitable at Biltmore within the next ten years, I shall consider you the wisest forester and financier of the age." [10]

During his first two years at Biltmore Pinchot was fortunate in finding a ready market for cordwood and sawed lumber on the estate itself, where large quantities of wood were needed for the kilns of the brickworks, maintenance of a branch railroad running to Biltmore House, and various construction projects. Because of this situation the forestry work by the end of 1893 showed a favorable financial balance. During that year receipts for wood and lumber sold and the value of wood on hand amounted to $11,324.19. Expenses for the work (exclusive of his own salary) amounted to $10,103.63.[11] Thus Pinchot was able to announce "a balance of $1,220.56 on the side of practical Forestry — conservative lumbering that left a growing forest behind

---

[9] Pinchot to Brandis, February 25, 1892, GPP.
[10] B. E. Fernow to Pinchot, September 19, 1892, Letters Sent by the Division of Forestry, RG 95.
[11] Report of Pinchot's forest assistant, C. L. Whitney, January 10, 1894, GPP.

it." [12] These cuttings were continued for several years thereafter and produced annually about 3,000 cords of firewood. This wood was sold in competition with that taken by neighboring farmers from their lands with traditional lumbering methods and it brought a fair margin of profit above the cost of cutting and hauling. Meanwhile the general condition of the Biltmore Forest showed steady improvement. The beneficial effects of the cuttings, however, were doubtless made possible to some extent by the exclusion of cattle from the forest land and the adoption of fire prevention methods. [13]

The forest experiment at Biltmore was given its initial large-scale publicity in the exhibit and pamphlet which, as part of his contract with Vanderbilt, Pinchot had agreed to prepare in connection with the World's Columbian Exposition at Chicago in 1893. The Biltmore Forest Exhibit seems to have been the first formal display of scientific forestry ever made in the United States. With large photographs and maps, the nature of the woodland and its improvement under scientific management were illustrated. Models of well-managed European forests detailed plans of future work. The pamphlet described the physical characteristics of Biltmore Forest, forestry practices inaugurated in it, and receipts and expenditures for the first year's work. The exhibit and pamphlet evoked much favorable comment. Vanderbilt praised his young forester and authorized him to order and distribute 10,000 copies of the pamphlet "for the good of the [forestry] cause." [14] An editorial in *Garden and Forest*, the most influential forest magazine in America during the 1890's, asserted that the Biltmore pamphlet marked "what must be considered a most important step in the progress of American civilization, as it records the results of the first attempt that had been made on a large scale in America to manage a piece of forest property on the scientific principles which prevail in France, Germany, and other European countries." [15]

The Exposition of 1893, in addition to the publicity for the Biltmore Forest experiment, also gave Pinchot the opportunity to highlight in a second exhibit the impressive forest resources of North Carolina and their need for protection. Describing the area to Sir Dietrich Brandis, he had written earlier, "North Carolina happens to be so situated that

---

[12] *Breaking New Ground*, p. 54.
[13] Overton W. Price, "Practical Forestry in the Southern Appalachians," *Yearbook of the United States Department of Agriculture, 1900* (Washington, 1901), p. 364.
[14] Vanderbilt to Pinchot, October 11, 1893, GPP.
[15] *Garden and Forest*, vii (February 21, 1894), 71.

the Northern and Southern floras meet within the State. There is no other state in the union where so many of the valuable kinds of trees are found."[16] And to Fernow he had described a belt of poplar on lands of the Cherokee Indians near Waynesville as "the finest strip of deciduous forest" that he had seen.[17] Against such a background of appreciation of the state's forests, the State Geologist, Joseph A. Holmes, and possibly other state officials, had no difficulty in persuading Pinchot to prepare a state forestry exhibit for the Exposition. Not only did this second display, too, make a good impression,[18] but the project also marked the beginning of a lasting friendship between Pinchot and Holmes. Their later collaboration was influential in the ultimate establishment of national forests in the Southern Appalachians.

Thus far, the Biltmore forest work had been confined mainly to timber cutting operations. In the spring of 1895, however, Pinchot directed the planting near Biltmore House of seedlings of yellow poplar, black cherry, tulip tree, black walnut, and a few other species. Due largely to unfavorable weather conditions the project was a failure. But other species planted on the estate with similar methods in later years grew to maturity and definitely showed the practicality of large-scale reforestation by private forest owners. The results of this work were to become the object of special study by the Appalachian Forest Experiment Station during 1921 and 1922.[19] Meanwhile Pinchot collected seeds from many parts of the world for the Biltmore Arboretum which was planned "not merely to make a botanical collection, but to show the value of trees as elements both in scenery and in practical Forestry."[20] It was to include 300 acres of 100 of the most valuable and hardy forest species. In a few years the Biltmore Arboretum actually came to possess the most complete collection of forest flora in the southeastern United States and had more woody plants than the world-famous Royal Botanical Gardens in London. Despite Pinchot's pleas for its continuance, however, Vanderbilt failed to make permanent provision for the arboretum.

While Pinchot was experimenting with scientific forestry on the Biltmore Estate, he began to examine large forest tracts near the estate

---

[16] Pinchot to Brandis, February 25, 1892, GPP.

[17] Pinchot to Fernow, February 14, 1893, Letters Received by the Division of Forestry, RG 95.

[18] J. A. Holmes to Pinchot, September 19, 1893, GPP.

[19] See Ferdinand W. Haasis, *Forest Plantation at Biltmore, North Carolina* (U.S.D.A. Miscellaneous Publication No. 61, Washington, 1930), 30 pp.

[20] *Breaking New Ground*, p. 55.

which his rich employer sought for use as a vast game preserve and camping ground. This work brought him to the Pink Beds, a great valley tract of unusual natural beauty covered by thickets of the laurel and rhododendron whose pinkish blossoms gave the site its name. He was certain the area would be ideal for hunting and camping and with the exclusion of cattle and fire would offer promise for scientific forestry. There were virgin stands of yellow poplar, hemlock, hickory, black walnut, beech and a good number of seed-bearing trees. In the spring of 1894 another survey trip carried him to a large mountainous tract northeast of the Pink Beds which was covered with a mature growth of chestnut, oak, and yellow poplar more beautiful than any he had seen in North Carolina. The reckless lumberman's ax had never threatened its primeval splendor. Here was another potentially fruitful field for forest management, and with this realization Pinchot immediately made tentative preparations for such an undertaking. His plans included an estimate of readily removable timber, recommendation of a fence law against forest trespassers, employment of forest guards, and the building of fire lines and trails. Most of these proposals, though new to American lumbering in 1894, within a few years were to become standard elements in American forest management.

The tracts beyond the Biltmore Estate surveyed by Pinchot were purchased early in 1895 and Vanderbilt consolidated them to form the Pisgah Forest. From the headwaters of the French Broad River this woodland extended southward over some 100,000 acres. Close examination of its mature timber had convinced Pinchot that extensive cutting would facilitate natural reproduction of the trees. Therefore, he designed a plan to facilitate harvesting of the mature forest crop and at the same time to let in vital light for the growth of seedlings — the bases for future crops. Vanderbilt approved the plan and the first cutting was done in October 1895, in what was perhaps the first systematic attempt in American lumbering to secure the natural reproduction of a forest area. Although it did not produce immediate financial profit, it pointed the way to more rational use and protection of forest resources. By 1914 the site of Pinchot's logging operations in Pisgah Forest was considered to have a silvicultural condition "unequaled elsewhere in the Southern Appalachians." A young growth of "remarkable density" had sprung up under the old trees, and virtual restoration of primeval forest conditions had been accomplished.[21] By

---

[21] Overton W. Price, "George W. Vanderbilt, Pioneer in Forestry," *American Forestry*, xx (June 1914), 422.

1930 a new forest crop was ready for commercial logging. The hope of Pinchot, Holmes, and others had meanwhile become a reality when this great forest tract was acquired in 1916 by the United States Government to form the Pisgah National Forest. In a letter offering the forest for government purchase, Mrs. George W. Vanderbilt in 1914 had aptly described its historic importance: "I wish earnestly to make such disposition of Pisgah Forest as will maintain in the fullest and most permanent way its national value as an object lesson in forestry, as well as its wonderful beauty and charm."[22]

As a whole, Pinchot undoubtedly enjoyed his experience at Biltmore and considered it highly profitable. But his endeavors were not without some disappointment and conflict, and he was to find that the significance of his work was not always fully appreciated by the owner of the Biltmore Estate. In 1892, Pinchot could write to Brandis, "Mr. Vanderbilt recognizes as fully as I do the educational value of the work and is disposed to do everything to give that side of it prominence and force."[23] But early in 1895, again writing to Brandis, he complained, "The scientific value of this place does not seem to appeal to Mr. Vanderbilt as much as it did, nor as far as I can see does he realize at all the ways in which a useful result in this direction is to be obtained. In a word, Biltmore is taking its position in his mind as his own pleasure ground and country seat with very secondary reference to its usefulness in other directions."[24] Some of the later feeling probably grew from Vanderbilt's lack of interest in expanding and continuing the arboretum project. The attitude could be traced, Pinchot thought, to some of Vanderbilt's advisers whom he considered "men incapable of appreciating the scientific point of view."[25] One of the advisers he had in mind was probably Charles McNarnee, general manager of the estate, with whom he had experienced difficulties in getting approval for forestry expenditures. Moreover, in establishing management over Vanderbilt's vast forest domain he sometimes had to challenge the trespassing of mountaineers who farmed, grazed cattle, hunted, fished, and "stilled" now and then within its boundaries.

Pinchot's direct supervision of the forestry work in Biltmore and

---

[22] Edith S. Vanderbilt (Mrs. George W. Vanderbilt) to the Secretary of Agriculture, May 1, 1914, Weeks Forestry Act Case Files, Record Group 16, Records of the Office of the Secretary of Agriculture, National Archives.

[23] Pinchot to Brandis, February 2, 1892, GPP.

[24] Pinchot to Brandis, January 24, 1895, GPP.

[25] Pinchot to Brandis, January 24, 1895, GPP.

Pisgah Forests ended in 1895. Not only did he now feel that the work had expanded to the extent of requiring the service of a full-time-resident forester but ventures in other parts of the United States were also claiming much of his time. Thus, on his recommendation Vanderbilt in the spring of 1895 hired a well-trained German forester, Carl A. Schenck, to have immediate supervision of the forestry work, while Pinchot kept general direction of the work. Despite some differences of opinion concerning particular silvicultural methods best suited for American forests, the two foresters cooperated in planning and directing the Biltmore and Pisgah operations. This association, however, gave way a few years later to distrust and hostility when Pinchot questioned the advisability of continuing the Biltmore Forest School founded by Schenck.[26]

By 1898, when Pinchot left Vanderbilt's service to accept appointment as Forester in the United States Department of Agriculture, the Biltmore Estate had become widely known as a center of forestry. College graduates increasingly were seeking training and experience in its woodlands and forest school. It had become a mecca for advocates of scientific forestry and forest preservation. Bernhardt Ribbentrop, Inspector General of Forests of the Government of India, had visited Biltmore in 1895 and called Pinchot's work "a wonderful good operation — a perfect piece of work."[27] The following year Secretary of Agriculture J. Sterling Morton, the "father" of Arbor Day, took "great satisfaction in going over the Forestry work" on the estate.[28] During the same year R. H. Warder, Superintendent of Cincinnati's Park Department, examined this work and lauded it as "a practical example to the whole country."[29]

The Biltmore Estate, now owned by grandsons of George W. Vanderbilt, is still being managed as a forest holding. Successful reforestation and timber cutting are carried on under the direction of a full-time forester. This first and continuing American example of effective scientific forestry helped to influence increasing numbers of private forest owners to adopt what Pinchot demonstrated at Biltmore to be practical and profitable — the management of forests for continuous timber crops.

[26] Pinchot to Vanderbilt, July 20, 1903, General Correspondence, RG 95.

[27] Cited in *Breaking New Ground*, p. 67.

[28] Secretary Morton to R. W. Furnas, March 12, 1896, Record Group 16, Records of the Office of the Secretary of Agriculture, National Archives.

[29] Warder to Charles A. Keffer, September 12, 1896, Letters Received by the Division of Forestry, RG 95.

V

Consulting Forester

EVEN WHEN HIS WORK in Vanderbilt's woodlands had been under way for scarcely two years, Pinchot was already looking for new fields. Thus, in December 1893 he had opened an office in Room 514 of the newly constructed United Charities Building on Fourth Avenue at Twenty-second Street, New York City, and placed upon the door the unique title, "Consulting Forester." For the next four and a half years, and while his association with Vanderbilt was continuing, Pinchot's New York office was to be the fountainhead of scientific forest management and the principal stimulus to the new profession of forestry in the United States. The State of New York thus again became the site of a pioneer step in the American forestry movement and furnished another leader in its development. Back in 1872, in advance of other states and the federal government, New York had instituted a beginning forest reserve policy by creating a commission to consider State ownership of wild lands north of the Mohawk River. The year 1885 saw these efforts rewarded when a permanent state forest commission was established to administer a forest reserve system. New York thereby gained the leadership in pioneering public forest administration.[1]

---

[1] The early history of forest policy in New York is traced in Herbert A. Smith, C. R. Tillotson, and Catherine M. O'Donnell, "State Accomplishments and Plans," *A National Plan for American Forestry* (73d Congress, 1st Sess., Senate Doc. No. 12, 1933), pp. 756–763.

A native of Connecticut, a well-known national conservationist, and a controversial figure in Pennsylvania politics, Pinchot has not often been thought of in connection with New York's history. Nevertheless, during the 1890's he was a voting resident of the State, a prominent participant in its civic life, and a leader in the movement to bring scientific forest management to the State. He lived with his parents at 2 Grammercy Park, New York City, as well as at the family's estate at Milford, Pennsylvania. By 1893 he had come to believe that his residence in the city with accessibility to many owners of large forest tracts provided an opportunity to broaden his forestry experience by offering forest management service to these persons. The practicability of such service may have become evident to him as early as October 1892, when he had been asked to make a preliminary examination of a large forest area in the Adirondacks owned by George Vanderbilt's brother-in-law, W. Seward Webb. The need for forest management on Webb's land was apparent from the survey, and it provided a means to introduce scientific methods into several areas of Adirondack woodlands then being acquired by men of wealth.

In addition to his services to private land owners who were seeking his scientific advice, the consulting forester had an early occasion to turn his special attention to the state-owned forest preserve in the Adirondacks. His concern here was to save the Adirondack forests from destructive use, which had begun with extensive lumbering of virgin pine, and by 1893 was resulting in widespread loss of commercially valuable spruce. In that year, New York Governor Roswell P. Flower obtained enactment of a law permitting the State Forest Commissioners to sell spruce and tamarack timber which was not less than twelve inches in diameter at a height of three feet above the ground, and poplar timber of such size as the Commissioners might determine. Now, as before, with little thought for future needs and no provision for growth of future timber crops, the devastation continued. Even forest lands of the State Preserve set aside in 1895 did not escape; they were being depleted because of defective titles as well as from depredations of lumber companies and other timber users.

Pinchot felt that this legalization of timber cutting on State lands without provision for its supervision by trained foresters would lead to further destruction of the State's forests. In addition, many sentimental defenders of forests, with whom Pinchot often disagreed, objected to timber cutting under any circumstances, lest it should spoil the rare scenic beauty of the Adirondack region and take away its value for health and recreational purposes. The ensuing considerable criticism of its administration moved the New York State Forest Commission — prompted by William F. Fox, Superintendent of State Forests — to hold a forestry meeting to discuss forest policy for the State, with special attention to the Adirondacks. On February 24, 1894, Pinchot accepted an invitation to address this meeting, which was planned with the cooperation of the American Forestry Association, New York Forestry Association, Adirondack Park Association, and Genesee Valley Forestry Association.

The forestry meeting, held at Albany from March 6 to 8, 1894, gave Pinchot an opportunity to be heard by several prominent advocates of forest preservation. Among these were J. Sterling Morton and Fernow from the federal government, J. T. Rothrock from Pennsylvania, and Morris K. Jessup and Warren Higley, influential in the New York Forestry Association. It was Pinchot's first major attempt to influence public policy concerning forests. Speaking on the subject "Forester and Lumberman in the North Woods," he strove to distinguish forestry from lumbering and show why the former was to be preferred for the general welfare of the State. In lumbering, he contended, the only objective was to get the largest profit out of an existing forest crop, while in forestry the aim was to get the largest return consistent with protecting and increasing the productive capacity of the forest. Accordingly, he maintained that the State should have in view not financial profit but preservation of favorable forest conditions, and should adopt forestry principles in the public interest. These principles could not be fulfilled by a restriction of the size of the trees to be cut which was not based upon a comprehensive plan for expert care of the forest.[2]

Pinchot's views were vigorously supported by Fernow and were adopted in resolutions of the Albany meeting. It soon became evident, however, that most people of the state wanted to preserve the Adirondack wilderness, with its mountains, lakes, and forests, as a great recreational area and were inclined to view timber cutting, even under forestry principles, as conflicting with this purpose. This attitude led to the inclusion in the State Constitution adopted on November 6, 1894, of a provision prohibiting any cutting from the State Forest Preserve. Although Pinchot realized that this provision was the result of the maladministration of the State's forests and that it gave some protection to them, he lamented that it "vetoed Forestry" on the Pre-

---

[2] Speech by Pinchot at Albany, March 7, 1894, GPP.

serve.[3] The result, to him, was like "the case of a farmer who should refuse to cultivate his farm on the ground that he distrusted his own fitness and integrity."[4] Despite the criticism of Pinchot and other foresters this constitutional prohibition against scientific forestry was to endure.

While Pinchot was urging the introduction of scientific forest management in the North Woods, his consultation services were in demand in other regions. During the greater part of 1894 and 1895, while he was still associated with George Vanderbilt, he planned and supervised forestry operations on Vanderbilt's extensive forest tracts in North Carolina. William G. Mather, president of the Cleveland-Cliffs Iron Company sought his advice on problems of forest management for the company's lands in Marquette County, Michigan. The work of the consulting forester attracted the attention of an increasing number of advocates of forest preservation. Among these was Theodore Roosevelt, then a member of the United States Civil Service Commission, who within the next decade was to become the most famous advocate of all. In 1894 Roosevelt had become acquainted with Pinchot's forestry projects and was beginning to respect his views. After a conversation with him in Washington, D.C., on May 21, the future President in a subsequent letter remarked with characteristic enthusiasm: "I did not begin to ask you all the questions I wanted to."[5]

Meanwhile Pinchot's activities were obviously arousing interest in forestry as a profession. By June 1894 many persons were coming to his New York office to confer about the training and occupational opportunities in this new field, and in Washington similar inquiries were being received in growing numbers by the Division of Forestry. This federal agency began to cite Pinchot as a successful example and suggest the availability of more information from his office. His accomplishments undoubtedly influenced Henry S. Graves, a friend and fellow alumnus of Yale University, to become the second American to choose forestry as a profession.

During the summer and autumn of 1894, Graves under Pinchot's supervision made a study of white pine in woodlands of central Pennsylvania and Franklin and Clinton Counties, New York. Financed by D. Willis James, William E. Dodge, and James W. Pinchot, the enterprise was intended to show the essential nature of forestry, stimu-

---

[3] *Breaking New Ground*, p. 70.
[4] Pinchot to Thomas H. Wagstaff, December 10, 1896, GPP.
[5] T. Roosevelt to Pinchot, May 22, 1894, GPP.

late similar investigation elsewhere, and above all to facilitate and hasten "the general introduction of right methods of forest management." Only through such management could American forests be saved.[6] The white pine study completed in 1896 was regarded as a pioneering American investigation and brought Pinchot's efforts into greater prominence. Fernow, although criticizing the study from the standpoint of methodology, did admit that it outlined "the proper direction" for American forestry investigations.[7]

As his work and recognition grew, Pinchot was ever more convinced that he had chosen the right profession. When his grandfather, Amos R. Eno, offered him a place in his business, Pinchot declined, and wrote of the occasion, "I find it impossible . . . to abandon my profession as a forester, both on account of the engagements already made and the opportunities which I believe it affords." He was convinced not only that he could go far but that he could go to the top. His buoyancy of spirit led him to regard prophetically the job of consulting forester as "training for Head Forester of the United States."[8]

Undoubtedly reinforcing Pinchot's optimism was the emerging interest within educational institutions, as educators began to turn to him for advice on setting up courses in forestry instruction. Among them was President Seth Low of Columbia University, who knew Pinchot as a member of his Bible Class at St. George's Episcopal Church. In January 1895 President Low was furnished an outline of a two-year forestry program for college graduates trained in political economics, mathematics, botany, geology, physics, and German or French. The outline recommended that before entering the course, students spend at least two months in the woods to gain some familiarity with forest growth.[9] A few months later the consulting forester's client was S. Bayard Dod, president of the Forestry Association of New Jersey, who wanted to establish a forestry school at Princeton University.[10] About the same time he conferred with N. L. Britton, director of the New York Botanical Gardens, concerning a proposed forest school. Although neither of these projects did materialize, the planning connected with

[6] Gifford Pinchot and Harry S. Graves, *The White Pine* (New York, 1896), p. vii.

[7] Fernow to Frank F. Nicola, December 3, 1896, Letters Sent by the Division of Forestry, RG 95.

[8] Pinchot to James B. Reynolds, August 13, 1894, GPP.

[9] Pinchot to Low, January 18, 1895, GPP.

[10] Dod to Fernow, June 9, 1895, Letters Received by the Division of Forestry, RG 95.

them brought to the attention of more people the importance of forestry, and helped to accelerate its eventual introduction in educational institutions in New York and elsewhere. And the plans did serve in clarifying Pinchot's thinking about forestry education which was to provide the principal stimulus to the founding of Yale University's School of Forestry in 1900.

Favorable news concerning New York's consulting forester had spread to New Jersey by October 1895, when he was engaged as a consultant for the state government. He was asked "to prepare a report on the forestry question in the State and the adaptability of the several large divisions of the State to timber culture or scientific forestry." [11] Pinchot visited the principal forest districts of New Jersey and obtained valuable technical assistance from Henry Graves. His report described existing methods of fighting forest fires in New Jersey, suggested better methods, proposed a State forest protection organization, presented the effects of forest fires, and described the State's remaining timber resources. He likened the problem of forest fires to that of slavery which he contended might be shelved for a time at enormous cost but sooner or later had to be met. State Geologist John C. Smock appraised the report as an important contribution to knowledge of the State's forests and their damage by fires.[12]

Along with all his other activities, the ambitious consulting forester still found time to direct a project destined to have a significant influence on forestry in general, as well as specifically on private forestry in the Adirondacks. Pinchot had already made a preliminary survey, in 1892, of the forest lands of W. Seward Webb.[13] Now the objective was preservation and proper management of spruce trees on these lands, which were a part of a tract of 40,000 acres called Ne-Ha-Sa-Ne Park, in Hamilton and Herkimer Counties. Traversed in a northeasterly direction by the Adirondack and St. Lawrence Railroad, bounded on the east by Little Tupper Lake and on the west by Big Rock Lake, the tract also included a portion of the headwaters of the Beaver River.

By March 1896, the examination of Ne-Ha-Sa-Ne Park was under way. Working sometimes in four feet of snow Pinchot, assisted by his

[11] Geological Survey of New Jersey, *Annual Report of the State Geologist, 1895* (Trenton, 1896), p. xxxii.

[12] Geological Survey of New Jersey, *Annual Report of the State Geologist, 1898* (Trenton, 1899), p. xxviii.

[13] Webb, brother-in-law of George W. Vanderbilt, in 1896 was head of the St. Lawrence and Adirondack Railway, Rutland Railroad and Raquette Lake Railway Companies.

friend Henry Graves and a few forest workers, closely surveyed the Park's forest resources. Webb's property appeared to be quite adaptable to management. Dominated by commercially valuable spruce and other hardwoods, the area never had been lumbered extensively. Unlike many other vast tracts in the Adirondacks, it had escaped the ravages of the charcoal-burning furnaces of the iron industry which sometimes had swept away trees as though "some gigantic scythe bearer" had mowed them.[14] Nor had the Park suffered as much as adjacent areas from the destruction of forest fires caused by the neglect of private and public owners.

The working plan that Pinchot formulated from the Ne-Ha-Sa-Ne Park survey, which was completed by the end of 1897, was to become a model for other American foresters. Especially noteworthy in the plan was a statement of rules for the cutting of timber which emphasized the forester's authority in the marking and cutting of trees, stipulated fire prevention measures, stressed protection of young growth, and provided penalties to lumbermen for noncompliance with the rules. The Park survey also provided data for Pinchot's book, *The Adirondack Spruce*. The first American book to give a detailed plan for the management of a particular forest, it was an important incentive for the application of forestry principles to American conditions. Distributed widely among owners of forest lands in the Adirondacks, the book was received and read with great interest.

The work of Pinchot and Graves at Ne-Ha-Sa-Ne Park had, in the following year, attracted the attention of William C. Whitney, former Secretary of the Navy, who owned a tract of 68,000 acres adjoining the Park. Consequently, Whitney agreed to an experiment in forestry on his lands. In general, the work of the two pioneer foresters in the woodlands of Webb and Whitney consisted of the careful preparation of timber estimates and maps and the drafting of contracts prohibiting lumbermen from cutting spruce trees less than ten inches in diameter. It provided for the preservation of some large trees for seed and the cutting of other merchantable trees without restriction to size.

With some variations, forestry operations on the Webb and Whitney estates have continued along the general lines recommended by Pinchot and Graves.[15] These operations have produced profits better than the

---

[14] L. E. Chittenden, *Personal Reminiscences, 1840–1890* (New York, 1893), p. 162.

[15] William M. Foos, Director, Lands and Forests, New York Conservation Department, to Harold T. Pinkett, March 13, 1956.

average for Adirondack forest properties.[16] The chief value of the operations, however, was as an object lesson of the practicability and profitability of scientific forestry. Two years after logging had begun at Ne-Ha-Sa-Ne the manager of the estates reported to Pinchot: "I have heard only good words lately for cutting timber under forestry supervision as instituted by you, and I cannot imagine Dr. Webb going back to the old careless methods."[17] The success of this work in the Adirondacks so impressed Pinchot that he was encouraged to continue and expand it as his career in forestry progressed.

In the course of his various enterprises and ventures in the cause of forestry, the larger compass of the public domain had continued to occupy a great deal of Pinchot's attention and energies. The American forest issue of the 1890's — the preservation and use of the nation's rapidly dwindling forests — had been kept alive for more than a decade by leaders of the American Forestry Association, including such New York stalwarts as Franklin Hough, Bernhard Fernow, and Warren Higley. It had been discussed at the 1894 Albany forestry meeting which Pinchot addressed, and where he joined representatives of various associations in adopting resolutions urging upon the President and Congress "the pressing necessity of an immediate and thorough inquiry into the scientific, commercial, climatic, and economic bearings of the forestry question . . . to establish a systematic and permanent policy concerning the national forests."[18] On December 16, 1894, Pinchot further explored the subject with a few friends at New York's famous Brevoort House on Fifth Avenue. In the group were Professor Charles S. Sargent, publisher of the influential journal *Garden and Forest*; William A. Stiles, editor of Sargent's journal; and Robert U. Johnson, an associate editor of the *Century Magazine*. They agreed to recommend the appointment of a commission to study the public timberlands and authorized Pinchot to outline the details for such a commission in a proposal to Congress. The young forester's plan called for the President to appoint a commission of three men who should examine the public forest areas, determine sites to be kept as forests, and propose a system for their scientific management. During 1895 he explained this plan to the New York Chamber of Commerce and New

---

[16] Hardy L. Shirley, "Large Private Holdings in the North," *Yearbook of Agriculture* (Washington, 1949), pp. 257–258.

[17] Edward M. Burns to Pinchot, May 31, 1900. General Correspondence, RG 95.

[18] Petition of the American Forestry Association, March 7, 1894, Record Group 46, Records of the United States Senate, National Archives.

York Board of Trade and Transportation and received their support.[19] Meanwhile, despite some opposition by Fernow, he won approval of the commission plan by the American Forestry Association.[20] Largely as a result of the efforts of Johnson, Stiles, Sargent, and Pinchot, the commission proposal was accepted by Hoke Smith, Secretary of the Interior, who in February 1896 called upon the National Academy of Sciences to report on "the inauguration of a rational forest policy" for the forests of the public domain. Specifically the Secretary sought the advice of the Academy on the following questions:

> (1) Is it desirable and practicable to preserve from fire and to maintain permanently as forested lands those portions of the public domain now bearing wood growth, for the supply of timber?
> (2) How far does the influence of forest upon climate, soil, and water conditions make desirable a policy of forest conservation in regions where the public domain is principally situated?
> (3) What specific legislation should be enacted to remedy the evils now confessedly existing?[21]

The National Academy, as we have seen, responded promptly to this request by the appointment of a committee (popularly known as the National Forest Commission) composed of seven able men. Among them was Gifford Pinchot, whose unique professional training, pioneering work, and enthusiasm had brought him at an early age to the forefront of a movement seeking to deal with one of America's most pressing public issues.

---

[19] *Breaking New Ground*, p. 87.

[20] Fernow apparently believed that the appointment of a Commission would delay the passage of pending legislation which sought to provide some degree of management of the public forests. See Andrew D. Rodgers, III, *Bernhard Eduard Fernow* (Princeton, 1951), p. 220.

[21] Fifty-fifth Congress, 1st Sess., Senate Doc. No. 105, p. 7.

VI

A Search for a Forest Policy

For MORE than a decade after his appointment to the National Forest Commission in 1896, the story of Gifford Pinchot's career is a dominant theme in the history of a great movement. It is the story of a pre-eminent role in a concerted effort initially to develop, dramatize, and sustain a program for the protection and rational use of forests, which expanded to an effort for the conservation of all the natural resources of the United States. It is the story of an heroic performance in an effort to show the American people how and why they should preserve these fundamental sources of their prosperity and safety.

From the beginning, Pinchot assumed a leading role in the work of the National Forest Commission. At its first meeting on April 21, 1896, he was appointed its secretary and with Arnold Hague was named on a committee to make a preliminary report and recommendation. He and other members of the Commission received valuable assistance from officials of the Interior and Agriculture Departments. Still more effective was the ardent support and practical advice from President Grover Cleveland, who urged them to consider the organization of a forest service, creation of more forest reserves, and preparation of proposed legislation in consultation with someone thoroughly familiar with the temper of Congress. In their preliminary report Pinchot and Hague earnestly recommended favorable consideration of Cleveland's suggestions and stressed the need for trained assistants to help the Commission prepare thorough studies of the public timberlands.

To Pinchot's disappointment, however, Chairman Sargent of the Commission refused to authorize the employment of trained assistants, and funds for the Commission's field work were delayed. Thus it was that Pinchot, at his own expense, hired Henry S. Graves as an assistant, and on June 1, 1896, started for the Northern Rocky Mountains to begin field work.[1] Other members of the Commission joined him in the field in July and together for three months they visited federal forest areas in Montana, Idaho, Oregon, California, Arizona, New Mexico, and Colorado. With them was John Muir, the famous naturalist and advocate of forest preservation. Being "tenderfeet," most of the commission members made the greater part of the journey by train and obtained what Pinchot regarded as rather superficial knowledge of the forest conditions. Though he and Graves were "tenderfeet" too, these two trained foresters chose to travel by horseback with pack outfits, thus being able at first hand to study some of the characteristics of the trees and note effects of fire, lumbering, and grazing on the wooded areas.

Meanwhile, President Cleveland had requested the National Forest Commission to report on a plan of federal forest management by November 1, 1896, so that he might examine and mention it in his December message to Congress. Despite the pleas of Pinchot and Hague, the Commission failed to submit such a plan at this time and recommended instead the creation of thirteen new forest reserves, the descriptions of which had been worked out by Pinchot. In submitting this recommendation to the President, David R. Francis, who had succeeded Hoke Smith as Secretary of the Interior, suggested that "the birth of the Father of our Country could be no more appropriately commemorated than by the promulgation by yourself of proclamations establishing these grand forest reservations."[2]

Thus on Washington's Birthday, February 22, 1897, Cleveland, whose administration was ending in ten days, created thirteen additional forest reserves comprising 21,279,840 acres situated in South Dakota, Wyoming, Montana, Idaho, Washington, California, and Utah. This action, taken without consultation with representatives of the states affected and without the announcement of a plan for the

---

[1] An appropriation of $25,000 was made in the sundry civil bill approved by Congress on June 11, 1896 (20 Stat., 432) to provide for the expenses of the National Forest Commission. The appropriation did not become available, however, until July 1, 1896.

[2] 55th Congress, 1st Sess., Senate Doc. No. 105, p. 39.

use of the resources of the reserves, was bitterly opposed by the West and threatened for a while to destroy the whole program of federal forest reservation. Just as the West had responded negatively in Harrison's administration, so now, several western Congressmen considered this measure a restriction on the development of the West, and they became permanent enemies of federal forest policy and its outgrowth, the conservation movement.

Opposition to the creation of the thirteen additional forest reserves had been especially strong in the Senate, which, on February 28, 1897, passed an amendment to an appropriation bill to nullify Cleveland's proclamations and restore the reserves to the public domain. Support for the reserves, however, was mustered in the House of Representatives which a few days later passed an amendment to authorize the Secretary of the Interior to sell timber in public forests and to make regulations necessary for the proper management and protection of the forests. (This provision was essentially what Pinchot had desired the National Forest Commission to recommend in its initial report to the President.[3] Eventually, it was to be the law under which the national forest system was to operate.) These conflicting amendments from the Senate and House were compromised in a measure which gave the President power to keep or cancel all or any part of any reserve. Cleveland, however, refused to sign the bill containing this compromise, and the reserve question was thus inherited by the McKinley administration.

Largely through the efforts of Charles D. Walcott, director of the United States Geological Survey, enough influential Congressmen were induced finally to support a forest reserve measure which had the approval of President William McKinley.[4] This measure, enacted on June 4, 1897, upheld the power of the President to create reserves under the act of 1891 but provided that no public forest reserve should be established "except to improve and protect the forest" or to secure "favorable conditions of water flow, and to furnish a continuous supply of timber for the use and necessities of citizens of the United States." All the reserves that had been proclaimed by Cleveland in February 1897, except those in California, were suspended and opened to private appropriation until March 1, 1898. The Secretary of the Interior was

---

[3] *Breaking New Ground,* p. 110.

[4] Walcott was doubtless strongly motivated in his efforts by the provision of the measure which granted $150,000 to the Geological Survey for surveying the forest reserves.

to have charge of the reserves and was empowered to make regulations necessary for the protection and use of the forests.[5]

At the same time that Congress was in process of settling the fate of the forest reserves, the National Forest Commission was having its own difficulties in formulating its final recommendations, as was noted earlier. Chairman Sargent and Abbot, the Army engineer, favored military control over the reserves, while Pinchot, Brewer, and Hague wanted civilian control through an organization of trained foresters. On May 1, 1897, six months after Cleveland had asked for it, and now into the McKinley administration, the Commission finally presented its report. Articulating a policy of rational use which Pinchot had urged at the outset, it declared: "A study of the forest reserves in their relations to the general development and welfare of the country, shows that the segregations of these great bodies of reserved lands can not be withdrawn from all occupation and use, and that they must be made to perform their part in the economy of the nation."[6]

The Commission maintained that the existing methods and forces at the disposal of the Interior Department were entirely inadequate to protect the public forests from destructive lumbering and grazing and the havoc of fire. It therefore recommended the establishment of a forestry bureau in the Department and the use of the army for protective measures until such a bureau could be formed. In reply to the first of the three specific questions it had been asked by Secretary Hoke Smith, the Commission contended that it was "not only desirable but essential to national welfare to protect the forested lands of the public domain." To the second question it replied that while forests probably do not increase the precipitation of moisture in any broad sense, they are necessary for the prevention of destructive floods and periods of low water. In answer to the third question the Commission submitted bills designed to provide for temporary military control of the reserves, a board to select new reserves, and lieu-land selections.[7]

Pinchot had been only partially satisfied with the achievements of the National Forest Commission. He especially deplored the fact that

---

[5] Act of June 4, 1897 (30 Stat. L., 11, 34, 35, 36).

[6] 55th Congress, 1st Sess., Senate Doc. No. 105, p. 22.

[7] Ibid., pp. 36–37. The lieu-land selections were intended to relieve settlers, who found their homesteads surrounded by a forest, by enabling them to exchange their land for a tract elsewhere in the unreserved public domain. Actually, the selections as provided for in the Act of June 4, 1897, mentioned above, led to widespread trading of worthless railroad grants and denuded timberlands for valuable unreserved tracts on the public domain.

a proposal for a rational forest policy had not been submitted in conjunction with the Commission's recommendation for more reserves, at the end of 1896. When Western opposition was heard following Cleveland's creation of the forest reserves early in 1897, Pinchot blamed it on Sargent's failure to make clear that the additional reserves were intended not to lock up more natural resources from all access, but rather to provide for their protection and rational use.[8] The American Forestry Association also had objected to increase of forest reserves without a satisfactory forest management policy. Fernow, one of the Association's most influential officers, later expressed his opinion that the National Forest Commission had nearly killed the government's reservation policy by its "stubborn disregard of public sentiment."[9] And now that the Commission had belatedly made its report to President McKinley, Pinchot believed that some of its proposals were inadequate or ill-advised, from the standpoint of scientific forestry. Nevertheless, despite his present misgivings and future regrets, he signed the Commission's report because he felt that it was at least an effective instrument for bringing the plight of the public timberlands to unprecedented national attention.[10]

Also brought to national attention by the Commission and its report was Gifford Pinchot. It established him as the foremost authority on American forest conditions. Thus, a few weeks after the Commission had ended its work, when Secretary of the Interior Cornelius Bliss needed someone to examine and report on the reserves suspended by the act of June 4, 1897, it was logical that he chose Pinchot for the job. Accordingly, the young forester on June 19, 1897, was appointed a special forest agent for the Department of the Interior at $10 per day and expenses. Only a year earlier Pinchot had surveyed western forest areas for the Commission. Now as a federal representative he was returning to the scene. During his examination of eighteen western reserves in the summer of 1897 he was thrilled by the sight of many magnificent bodies of woodland but equally appalled by many large forest tracts damaged by fire. He camped near and climbed Columbia Peak in the Washington Forest Reserve, an area of luxuriant forest growth which fifty-two years later was to be proclaimed as the Gifford Pinchot National Forest. He also conferred with and apparently

---

[8] *Breaking New Ground*, pp. 107–109.
[9] Fernow to Elwood Meade, January 11, 1898, Letters Sent by the Division of Forestry, RG 95.
[10] Pinchot to Walcott, May 6, 1897, GPP.

convinced some influential miners, ranchers, and newspaper editors as to the desirability of establishing forest reserves.

Reporting on his summer's work, Pinchot declared that the forest reserves then embracing an estimated area of some 38 million acres of forest and other lands had an enormous capacity for sustained production of wood that made their protection imperative. The great danger to their productive capacity and the national welfare, he observed, was not primarily the ax wielded in cutting timber for development of the country but, rather, uncontrolled forest fires that consumed vast stretches of timber without benefit to anyone. Therefore, the need was immediate for the establishment of permanent boundaries for the reserves and a professionally trained "forest service" organization to manage the reserve resources. The objectives of this management should be to maintain an effective fire control program, eliminate from the reserves the lands that were more valuable for agriculture than for forest purposes, regulate grazing uses in a flexible manner, and prescribe cutting operations to implement harvest of the largest amount of timber consistent with the steady improvement of the forests in fertility and usefulness. The possibility of attaining these goals, Pinchot reported, seemed greater than at any time since the outburst of public protest occasioned by Cleveland's creation of thirteen forest reserves. He believed that the outcry was diminishing with the spread of information concerning the government's liberal policy for the use of the reserves, but he stressed — as he tended to do increasingly in later years — the need for a greater publicity effort to reach great numbers of interested but uninformed users of forests.[11]

From his experiences as a member of the National Forest Commission and special forest agent for the Department of the Interior, Pinchot learned a great deal about the characteristics and economic value of American forests and the conditions that endangered their preservation and continued use. He found his new work exciting and challenging. Moreover, he had the opportunity to spend much time in the great woodland areas that he came to know and love so well. Here in hours off duty, he hunted, fished, camped, and listened to the fascinating adventure stories of John Muir and other companions. Here, too, he met and developed friendships with F. H. Newell, Henry L. Stimson,

[11] For Pinchot's report, see 55th Congress, 2d Sess., Senate Doc. No. 189, *Report on the Examination of the Forest Reserves* (Washington 1898), pp. 35–118.

and others who later were to be numbered among his staunchest supporters. In Washington this work gave him a chance to meet two
presidents, Cleveland and McKinley, and to become acquainted with
leaders in both branches of Congress and several prominent government officials. From them he learned something of administrative and
legislative processes and the bearing of public sentiment upon them.
Meanwhile he also came into close contact with older men, outside
the political arena, whose general knowledge of the United States and
experience in dealing with public figures and questions helped to shape
his views on forest and other resource issues.

VII

Federal Forester Without Forests

W HILE PINCHOT LABORED to convince the National Forest Commission of the urgency for a rational forest policy, the Forestry Division in Washington, which might have been expected to help him, was in trouble with Congress. The Division since its establishment in 1880 had functioned mainly as a bureau of information and had done nothing to formulate forest policy or encourage forest management. Finally, in 1898 Congress inserted into the agricultural appropriation a clause which in effect ordered the Division of Forestry to show why it should not be abolished. B. E. Fernow, the Division head, who had been skeptical of the practicability of Pinchot's work on the Vanderbilt timberlands, was equally doubtful of the feasibility of forest management work by the federal government. It was thus that Fernow resigned and on May 11, 1898, Secretary of Agriculture James Wilson invited Gifford Pinchot to become head of the Division of Forestry. The young forester seemed to be the only available person capable of saving the Division and inaugurating a program of practical government forestry. He accepted the Secretary's invitation and on July 1, 1898, became Chief of the Division. Since there was then no one in the federal government competent to prepare a forestry examination for his appointment, he was asked to make out questions for his own examination. But before he had a chance to answer the questions, President William McKinley issued an order placing him in the classified Civil Service. According to Pinchot, the Secretary gave

47

him a free hand to run the Division as he saw fit, including the right to appoint assistants and conduct work without fear of interference.[1]

When Pinchot entered the Division it had eleven employees and an annual appropriation of $28,500. It had two foresters. He was one; his friend and assistant, Henry S. Graves was the other. The Division was then housed in two rooms in the attic of the old red brick Agriculture Department Building. Pinchot's office was about the size of a hall bedroom. Divisional equipment was practically nil. The absence of a marking hatchet, a basic forestry tool, was clear proof to the new Chief that his predecessors had been doing no thinking about practical forestry. The division seemed to lack nearly everything it needed except Pinchot's will to succeed.

Since the national forest reserves in 1898 were still under the jurisdiction of the General Land Office in the Department of the Interior, the Agriculture Department's Forestry Division did not control a single acre of forests. Its new Chief, however, was determined that this situation should not deter his effort to spread the gospel of scientific forest management and to halt destructive forest use. This had been his essential aim as a private forester, and he proposed to maintain his objectives as a government forester. Since he was still a federal forester without federal forests — and instead of merely exhorting and viewing with alarm — Pinchot focused his attention on private timberland owners. Accordingly, on October 15, 1898, in a famous Circular No. 21 the Division of Forestry offered to help farmers, lumbermen, and other private forest land owners to make working plans for conservative lumbering, with directions for practical work, and to assist them in the woods. Owners of woodlots were offered help without cost, while owners of larger tracts were required to pay the expenses of government assistants while in the field and the cost of local workers.[2]

The proffered guidance received a hearty response from a number of timberland owners. Within a year 123 lumbermen, farmers, and others asked for direction in introducing forestry methods on a million and a half acres in thirty-five states. At the same time successful forest management was in actual operation on 100,000 acres.[3] Within ten

---

[1] *Breaking New Ground*, pp. 135–136.

[2] U.S.D.A., Division of Forestry, *Report of the Forester, 1899* (Washington, 1899), pp. 3–4. Annual reports of the Federal Forester are cited hereafter as *Report of the Forester* with the pertinent year.

[3] *Report of the Forester, 1899*, p. 4.

years Pinchot's agency received 938 formal applications for forest management assistance on nearly thirteen million acres from coast to coast and made examinations on some eight million acres. The total forest land surveyed lay mainly on large timber tracts but did include a considerable acreage of farm woodlots; these holdings in the aggregate formed a large part of the productive forest of the United States. Among the large owners participating in this program were William G. Rockefeller, Abram S. Hewitt, E. H. Harriman, the Great Northern Paper Company, and the Frederick Weyerhaeuser Timber Company. Several hundred additional requests for assistance could not be processed formally because of the lack of men and money.[4] It is of interest to note that Mrs. James Roosevelt, mother of Franklin D. Roosevelt, requested an examination of her woodlands at Hyde Park, New York, but apparently was unsuccessful in obtaining it.[5]

Despite its acceptance in many quarters, still there was mixed reaction to this program of government cooperation with private forest owners. Many owners welcomed the opportunity to have working plans prepared for their lands and readily conceded their theoretical soundness, but were not always readily convinced of their economic usefulness. Sir Dietrich Brandis criticized the plans on the basis that they were prepared too much in a wholesale manner for too many tracts and lacked sufficient detail.[6] Pinchot replied that the great objective to be accomplished then in America was to get a large number of forest owners all over the country to introduce forest management, and he added that even if the methods were "very rough," much more would be accomplished than if a few tracts were managed intensively.[7] The immediate financial results of the introduction of forestry methods were admittedly uncertain. Some five years later, one of Pinchot's assistants remarked that his bureau usually lacked accurate records of expenses and receipts for forests involved in the management assistance program.[8] One notable exception, however, was the 6,500-acre forest domain of the University of the South at Sewanee, Tennessee, inspected by Pinchot in 1898 and placed under a Forestry Division working plan in 1900. Seven years later the Vice-Chancellor

---

[4] U.S.D.A., *Annual Reports* (Washington, 1909), p. 78.
[5] J. G. Peters to Mrs. James Roosevelt, July 25, 1905, Office of State and Private Cooperation Correspondence, RG 95.
[6] Brandis to Pinchot, August 27, 1899, General Correspondence, RG 95.
[7] Pinchot to Brandis, November 22, 1899, General Correspondence, RG 95.
[8] Thomas H. Sherrard to Juba E. Rogers, February 20 and March 9, 1905, Office of State and Private Cooperation Correspondence, RG 95.

of the University reported that this tract had yielded for sale 3,141,021 board feet of logs, at a net profit of $12,969.41. In normal lumbering operations of the locality in 1900, he indicated, $2,000 would have been considered a fair valuation of the University's timber. But by 1907, the profitable logging had improved growth of young trees and reproduction of several species. Accordingly, the venture was hailed as an object lesson for the locality and the entire South.[9]

Although government assistance to private forest owners was curtailed after 1905, and regular reports on the project were no longer received, fragmentary data did disclose that some large timberland owners continued to follow program recommendations. A survey in 1911 showed that many of them were employing foresters, maintaining fire patrol systems, prescribing cutting of trees with diameter limits and provision for preservation of seeding trees, and carrying on extensive planting projects.[10] A decade later Forester William B. Greeley, head of the Forest Service, remarked: "Every little while I run across land owners who have been following recommendations made by the Forest Service in 1903 or 1904, with surprisingly good results."[11] More important than these direct results, probably, were the indirect educational effects. The management assistance program brought forestry out of the office and lecture hall and into the woods where it helped to convince more Americans that forest use and protection were not incompatible. It cast Pinchot and his assistants into the role of missionaries carrying the message of forestry to the private forest domain. In effect, therefore, it inaugurated government extension forestry, which a quarter of a century later was to become a major federal-state activity for promotion of better forest practice on private lands.

The Forestry Division's assistance to private forestry provided still another educational benefit. Young American foresters gained valuable experience as preparation for tasks which came to them a few years later when forest management was introduced on the national forest reserves and was sought increasingly for state as well as private tim-

---

[9] B. Lawton Wiggins to the Secretary of Agriculture, April 18, 1897, Office of State and Private Cooperation Correspondence, RG 95. Carl A. Schenck in his memoirs, *The Biltmore Story* (St. Paul, 1955), p. 81, has erroneously indicated that the University of the South failed to adopt a forest management program for its forest land.

[10] Unsigned memorandum titled "Private Interests Engaged in the Active Practice of Forestry," August 25, 1911, Research Compilation File, RG 95.

[11] Greeley to District Foresters and Forest Supervisors, April 5, 1924, Timber Management Division Correspondence, RG 95.

berlands. As this work expanded, Pinchot's staff of foresters grew. In addition to Henry Graves, the group enlarged to include men like Overton W. Price, Ralph Hosmer, William L. Hall, and Raphael Zon, who were to give long, able, and valuable reinforcement to Pinchot's efforts for forest conservation. Sometimes called "Pinchot's young men," they often gathered at the "Chief's" home after regular working hours for a "spread" of gingerbread, baked apples, and milk, and listened to inspiring talks to spur them on in their pioneer efforts. In addition, several promising foresters were recruited through the creation of a group of "student assistants" in the Division of Forestry. Most were college men who worked under the supervision of trained foresters in the preparation of working plans and the study of commercial trees, and received $25 per month.[12] Many of them were personally indebted to Pinchot who often helped them to get started at work by endorsing promissory notes for them drawn on Riggs National Bank in Washington.[13] Nearly all of them were ultimately imbued with the fierce determination and zeal of their "Chief" to halt the devastation of American forests.

A major opportunity for Pinchot to make a persuasive statement on forest preservation came in 1900 when, as a result of a request of the Secretary of the Interior to the Secretary of Agriculture, his Division was called upon for technical advice regarding the management of the national forest reserves. Pinchot obliged with an outline of principles and practices which he considered desirable in the administration of the reserves. Specifically, he advocated a wide extension of the western forest reserve area; measures to foster the good will and cooperation of residents in and near the reserves, especially in regard to the prevention of forest fires; promotion of conservational use by the people of all natural resources on the reserves; and the establishment of a decentralized system of forest administration.[14] These recommendations embodied fundamental principles upon which the national forest system would later be built. But the Interior Department's General Land Office, still custodian of the public timberlands, had little interest in the program and succeeded in preventing its acceptance. The request for advice did have one advantageous result, however.

---

[12] *Report of the Forester, 1899,* p. 3.
[13] Ralph S. Hosmer, "Some Recollections of Gifford Pinchot, 1898–1904," *Journal of Forestry,* XLIII (August 1945), 560.
[14] Pinchot to the Secretary of the Interior, October 31, 1901, Research Compilation File, RG 95.

It enabled Pinchot and his staff to investigate forest conditions in several federal reserves, whereby they further developed basic technical forest methods and acquired valuable information concerning the resources of the reserves. Also around the beginning of the century, several states, the first of which was New York, began to call upon the Forestry Division for technical assistance in the care of their forest lands. The appeals for professional guidance first from private owners and later from the federal and state governments gave encouragement and hope to all proponents of forest conservation.

Pinchot's knowledge of forests was also broadened by a visit to the Philippine Islands, late in October 1902, at the invitation of Capt. George P. Ahern, Chief to the Philippine Forestry Bureau, who had been an admirer of the young forester since meeting and working with him in Montana during the days of the National Forest Commission.[15] Shortly after his appointment to the Forestry Bureau in 1900, Ahern had sought Pinchot's views on forestry matters and declared that he would "reverence any suggestions" since he regarded Pinchot as the "greatest practical forester on God's Green Earth."[16] Now, during his 1902 trip, Pinchot studied the Islands' forest conditions and government forest organization and made recommendations for their improvement. In the course of some six weeks Pinchot found the forests of the Philippines to be "immensely rich in quality and amount of timber" and "admirably adapted for practical forestry," but in need of immediate protection against destructive lumbering operations. With Ahern's assistance he drew up proposals on forest policy, organization of the Forestry Bureau, conduct of forest business, and establishment of a Philippine forest school.[17] William H. Taft, who, in 1900 had been appointed the first civil governor of the Philippines, endorsed Pinchot's proposals, and these became a foundation of forestry in the Islands.[18]

Throughout these years near the turn of the century Pinchot was of course continuing his mission to create public awareness of the imperative necessity of his work. He stated:

---

[15] Lawrence Rakestraw, "Forest Missionary, George Patrick Ahern, 1894–1899," *Montana*, IX (October 1959), 36–44.

[16] Ahern to Pinchot, April 20, 1900, Letters Received by the Division of Forestry, RG 95.

[17] Gifford Pinchot, "Recommendations on Policy, Organization, and Procedure for the Bureau of Forestry of the Philippine Islands," *Report of the Philippine Commission*, Part 2 (Washington, 1904), pp. 315–325.

[18] S. B. Show, "American and World Forestry," in *Fifty Years of Forestry in the U.S.A.* (ed., R. K. Winters), (Washington, 1950), p. 344.

Young stand of Douglas spruce, Western hemlock and white fir in the Olympic National Forest, Washington, photographed by Gifford Pinchot in August 1897 during his investigations for the National Forest Commission.

(p. 44)

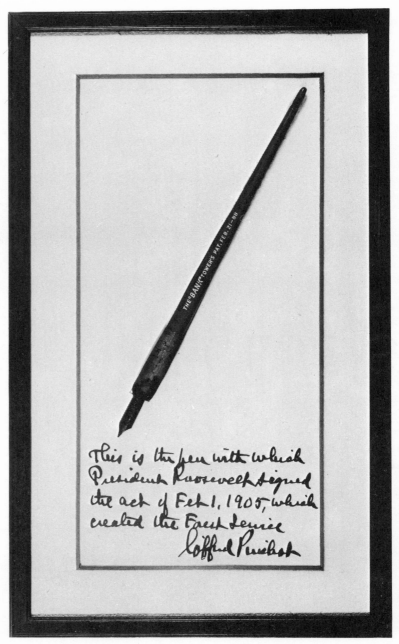

The pen with which President Theodore Roosevelt signed the Act of February 1, 1905, which created the Forest Service, with inscription by Gifford Pinchot, first Chief. (p. 57)

U.S. FOREST SERVICE

Nothing permanent can be accomplished in this country unless it is backed by a sound public sentiment. The greater part of our work, therefore, has consisted in arousing a general interest in practical forestry throughout the country and in gradually changing public sentiment toward a more conservative treatment of forest lands.[19]

As a part of this publicity effort he had lectured extensively and had written numerous articles for popular periodicals. In 1899 he published the first part of *A Primer of Forestry*, of which more than a million copies were eventually circulated by the federal government. To a botanist who accused him of using erroneous nomenclature for trees in this popular publication, Pinchot replied chidingly:

The object of this Division is not to bring the righteous, but sinners to repentance. Consequently, it matters little whether, botanically, the names we use are correct or not, while it is of the greatest importance that the practical men in whose hands the future welfare or destruction of the forest areas of this country must necessarily lie, should find themselves as much at home as possible in our publications.[20]

Even more influential than these publications were the good relations that the Division of Forestry established with the newspapers. It convinced them that forestry was news, and readily furnished them information about the Division's work to promote forestry, with the result that forestry news reached many more readers through newspaper items than through government publications.

Above all, Pinchot's efforts for forest conservation were strengthened from the very beginning by contact with and support of Theodore Roosevelt, in whom conservation was to find its most famous champion. In 1897 the Governor and future President sponsored the young forester's election to the Boone and Crockett, the club of big game hunters that he had founded.[21] Early in 1899 at Albany Pinchot had several conversations with Roosevelt and was gratified to note the Governor's realization of the importance of forestry. The Governor was heartily in

---

[19] Pinchot to R. C. Melward, May 20, 1903, Office of Forest Reserves Correspondence, RG 95.
[20] Pinchot to J. G. Lemmon, November 8, 1899, Letters Sent by the Division of Forestry, RG 95.
[21] *Breaking New Ground*, pp. 144–145.

favor of any well-planned effort for the protection and better management of the forests of New York.[22] Some months later the State Forest, Fish, and Game Commission appointed a few foresters on Pinchot's recommendation. Roosevelt seemed to be greatly impressed by the nonpartisan nature of the forester's ideas which he believed stemmed from the fact that Pinchot was no more influenced by politics in his work than, say, were the astronomers of the Harvard University Observatory.[23] Soon after his election to the Vice-Presidency in 1900, Roosevelt declared that there must be a wide extension of the national forest reserves and insisted that the whole prosperity and development of the West and indeed ultimately of the entire country are bound up with the preservation of forests.[24] After he became President in 1901, he was increasingly well-disposed toward Pinchot's advocacy of the conservation of forests and other natural resources and began to throw the influence of his office behind efforts for their protection. It was not difficult to arouse Roosevelt's interest in these efforts. Renowned as an outdoor enthusiast, he understood the language of forest and plain, river and mountain. As he listened to Pinchot, F. H. Newell, and a few other ardent conservationists, he could not only comprehend more of the beauty and mystery of nature, but also appreciate the potential value of forest-clad hills, tumbling streams, and arid plains.

In his first annual message to Congress on December 3, 1901, President Roosevelt enthusiastically proclaimed his support of the forestry policy, program and organization advocated earlier by Forester Pinchot.[25] Emphasizing that wise forest protection does not mean the withdrawal of forest reserves, whether involving wood, water, or grass, he urged the adoption of a policy that would enable the reserves to contribute their full share to the welfare of the people and give more assurance of future resources. He criticized the existing diffusion of responsibility for a federal forestry program, with protection of the national reserves resting with the General Land Office, the mapping and description of their timber with the Geological Survey, and the preparation of plans for their conservative use with the Bureau of

---

[22] Pinchot to Theodore Weston, March 9, 1899, Letters Sent by the Division of Forestry, RG 95.

[23] Elting E. Morison (ed.), *The Letters of Theodore Roosevelt* (Cambridge, Mass., 1951), II, 1320.

[24] Morison, II, 1421.

[25] The designation of "Chief of the Division of Forestry," was changed to "Forester" on July 1, 1899 (30 Stat. L., 949).

Forestry.[26] These various functions, he contended, should be consolidated in Pinchot's bureau, since it was charged with the general advancement of practical forestry and was staffed with qualified scientific personnel.[27] Considerable public support had already been engendered for this presidential recommendation. The unsatisfactory administration of the public timberlands by the General Land Office often had been pointed out. The following comment on the forest personnel of this office was typical: "It cannot be said of the force as at present constituted, that a little learning is a dangerous thing, as no one has accused any of these forest officials of the possession of any forestry information, either general or technical."[28] By 1901 many persons were convinced that Pinchot's bureau, because of its forestry-trained personnel and reputation for nonpartisanship, was the logical organization to have jurisdiction over the national forest reserves.

Three years later in a message to Congress Roosevelt reiterated his contentions about the national forest reserves and urged the transfer of all federal forest work to the Bureau of Forestry "in consonance with the plainest dictates of good administration and common sense."[29] Meanwhile he continued to rely heavily on Pinchot's counsel in determining the boundaries of proposed forest reserves. Largely on this advice he launched a program of federal forest preservation, unequaled in its extent before or since his time, so that by the close of his first presidential term the forty-six million acres of reserves created by his predecessors had been nearly doubled by his own efforts. These remnants of the once vast public domain lay in thirteen states and two territories and symbolized a new determination to save a valuable part of the national heritage.

Presidential contact and support in the interests of forestry were augmented by the prominence of Pinchot's role in the affairs of the American Forestry Association, of which he had been a member since college days at Yale. On March 3, 1904, at a meeting of a committee of his principal Bureau of Forestry assistants, he had presented a plan for a "Forest and Water Convention" to be held yearly in Washington,

---

[26] Pinchot's Division of Forestry was renamed Bureau of Forestry on March 2, 1901 (31 Stat. L., 929).

[27] James D. Richardson (ed.), *Messages and Papers of the Presidents, Supplement, 1899–1902* (New York), p. 328.

[28] Joseph B. Thoburn to Pinchot, October 6, 1898, General Correspondence, RG 95.

[29] Richardson (ed.), *Messages and Papers of the Presidents, Supplement, 1901–1905*, p. 842.

in early January, under the auspices of the American Forestry Association. Attendance would include federal forest and geological officials, forestry students, and representatives of private lumber and irrigation interests.[30]

Pinchot's plan for a "Forest and Water Convention" saw fruition in the convening of the American Forest Congress in Washington, D.C., January 2–6, 1905. Its general purpose was to discuss the necessity of forest preservation; its specific purpose was to rally support for the transfer of the federal forest reserves to the control of the Bureau of Forestry.

The American Forest Congress of 1905 was unique. As President Roosevelt declared in an address at the National Theatre on January 5, the Congress was without parallel in the history of American forestry, because it marked the first time that "the great business and forest interests of the nation" had joined together "to consider their individual and common interests in the forests." He then discussed the economic value of forest preservation and stressed the civic and moral responsibility of forest users to preserve resources for future generations.[31] Practical methods of safe-guarding the broad business interests of the nation, then threatened by forest devastation, were discussed by representatives of all the important industries dependent on forest use and by government officials. F. E. Weyerhaeuser, representing the Weyerhaeuser Lumber Company, announced that lumbermen were ready "to consider seriously any proposition which may be made by those who have the conservative use of the forests at heart." J. E. Defebaugh, editor of the *American Lumberman* suggested that Pinchot and other "disciples of forestry" had taken an important step forward "when they ceased to preach the doctrine of indirect and deferred benefits and began to demonstrate that direct benefits could be made to result from forestry as a science and as a practice."[32] F. H. Newell, Chief Engineer of the United States Reclamation Service, who was becoming increasingly allied with Pinchot's cause, and James J. Hill, President of the Great Northern Railway Company, stressed the interrelationship between forest preservation and irrigation.[33] Emphasizing the role that private owners of forests would have to assume if "the over-

---

[30] Minutes of the Service Committee, March 3, 1904, RG 95.

[31] U.S.D.A., Forest Service, Circular No. 35, *Forest Preservation and National Prosperity* (Portions of addresses delivered at the American Forest Congress, Washington, January 2–6, 1905), pp. 5–8.

[32] *Ibid.*, p. 25.

[33] *Ibid.*, pp. 12, 20.

whelming calamity of a timber famine" was to be averted, Pinchot called for reforestation measures and the extension of federal forest reserves not only on the public domain but also on land which might be acquired by purchase from private owners in the East and West.[34]

The sponsors of the American Forest Congress of 1905 regarded it as a very successful meeting. Outstanding was its adoption of resolutions favoring the unification of all government forest work in the Agriculture Department's Bureau of Forestry, purchase of reserves in the East, repeal of the Timber and Stone Act, and amendment of the lieu-land law. In general, it did much to fix attention on forest conservation as an extremely necessary national program.[35] Thanks to this development, sufficient support was mustered for the enactment of federal legislation on February 1, 1905, which transferred jurisdiction over the national forest reserves to the Department of Agriculture. This jurisdiction could then be vested in the Bureau of Forestry, with Pinchot in command. At last the way was open for the introduction of scientific measures for the protection and use of more than sixty-three million acres of public forests. To this task America's foremost disciple of forestry now eagerly turned his attention.

---

[34] *Ibid.*, p. 30.
[35] William L. Hall, "Hail to the Chief," *Journal of Forestry*, XLIII (August, 1945), 556.

VIII

Conservative Forest Use

WITH CONTROL of the national forest reserves transferred
to the Bureau of Forestry, conservation and development of all their
resources began in earnest. The scientific knowledge and public-spirited
zeal of Pinchot and his staff were turned to the task of opening the
door to the broadest utilization of these great areas for the satisfaction
of human needs. The purpose and goals of this undertaking were
guided by principles set forth in Secretary Wilson's letter of instruction to the Forester signed on the day the reserves were transferred.
In general, all land in the reserves was "to be devoted to the most productive use for the permanent good of the whole people, and not for
the temporary benefit of individuals or companies." Emphasis centered
on the idea that all forest resources are for use, although this use should
be regulated in such a manner as to insure the permanence of the
resources. Hence their "conservative use" would not injure their permanent value. More specifically, Chief Forester Pinchot was directed
to see that the water, wood, and forage of the reserves were conserved
and wisely used first for the benefit of the home builder and, second,
for the continued prosperity of agricultural, lumbering, mining, and
livestock interests. In the management of each reserve, local issues
were to be decided upon local considerations; the principal industry
should have first consideration but with as little restriction on other
industries as possible. Above all, where conflicting interests would
have to be reconciled, the issue should "always be decided from the

standpoint of the greatest good of the greatest number in the long run."[1]

Pinchot continually stressed that his administration of the nation's forest land was guided by a policy of conservative use. In prescribing administrative regulations he insisted:

> Forest reserves are for the purpose of preserving a perpetual supply of timber for home industries, preventing destruction of the forest cover which regulates the flow of streams, and protecting local residents from unfair competition in the use of forest and range. They are patrolled and protected at Government expense for the benefit of the community and the home builder.[2]

To help show that his administration was a service rather than a bureaucratic regime, he persuaded Congress to change the name of "Bureau of Forestry" to that of "Forest Service," effective July 1, 1905. To emphasize that the creation of reserves did not imply withdrawal of land from productive use, he also brought about in 1906 the change of the designation of "forest reserves" to that of "national forests." This change typified Pinchot's consistent attitude toward the purpose for which he deemed forests are managed — to secure the conservation of an essential natural resource in the national interest. The new designation was also an early indication of the strong national point of view that was to characterize so much of his thinking.

In accordance with the policy of conservative use, mature as well as dead timber was offered for sale wherever there was demand for it and the permanent care of the forest and protection of streams permitted its cutting.[3] Provision was made for its sale both in small and large quantities under regulations designed to prevent waste and fires, protect young growth, and insure reproduction. Timber sales amounting to more than $100 had to be advertised and approved by the For-

---

[1] Secretary Wilson to Pinchot, February 1, 1905, General Correspondence, RG 95. Pinchot stated that he prepared this important letter for Secretary Wilson's signature (see *Breaking New Ground*, p. 260). There is no reason to doubt this, since the letter contains basic principles long advocated by him before 1905 and often reiterated afterward.

[2] U.S.D.A., Forest Service, *The Use Book. Regulations and Instructions for the Use of the National Forest Reserves* (Washington, 1906), p. 13. This publication is cited hereafter as *Use Book*.

[3] The Act of June 4, 1897, mentioned earlier in this study (p. 42), authorized the sale of "dead, matured, or large growth of trees" on the federal forest reserves.

ester, but those up to $20 and $100 could be made by local forest rangers and supervisors, respectively. Timber sold had to be estimated and paid for before it was cut, and measured before it was moved. It could be cut only in the area designated by a forest officer and could include no green trees unless they had been marked officially for cutting. To prevent the common fraud of cutting live timber and paying for it as dead, the latter type was defined as "only timber, standing or down, which is actually dead, and in no case trees which are apparently dying."[4]

To aid western settlement by home makers, residents near the national forests were permitted to take $20 worth of timber yearly from the forests without charge, but under permits from forest officers.[5] This was no small privilege, for timber of this value might supply not only important needs for firewood, fencing, and mining but also suffice in some instances for the construction of a small house. Moreover, free use of timber was also granted to school and road districts, churches, and cooperative organizations, to an annual value of $100. In free use, as in timber sales, the protection of the forest was considered paramount. Cutting for any purpose was regulated to help prevent unnecessary damage and insure a future timber crop.

Pinchot's policy of conservative use also opened the way for regulated grazing in the national forests. In the early days of the reserves the wisdom of permitting any grazing upon them had been warmly debated. Pinchot's view was that the great quantity of grass and other forage plants on national forest land should be utilized under proper governmental regulations to prevent harm to young forest growth, water supplies, and the range itself through overuse or unwise methods of handling livestock. Consequently, he authorized grazing in all national forests unless the watersheds furnished water for domestic use. However, the amount of stock to be grazed by each applicant and the part of the range to be occupied were fixed under his supervision. In grazing, as in timber sales and free use, forest officers were directed to give first consideration to the needs of home builders.[6] President Roosevelt, who attached great importance to the grazing problem in the West and was opposed to the old free range system, enthusiastically endorsed the Forester's grazing policy.[7]

---

[4] *Use Book*, p. 49.
[5] *Use Book*, pp. 33–34.
[6] *Use Book*, p. 73.
[7] Roosevelt to Pinchot, November 27, 1905, Office of Organization Correspondence, RG 95.

Before the Forest Service was given control of the national forests, "stock wars" were common. Cattlemen, who nearly everywhere had first possession of the range, resented the coming of the sheep industry. Unscrupulous sheepmen often swept over a cattle range in a few weeks, their livestock practically destroying all its forage, before moving on to new fields. Since the public range theoretically was open and free for all, there was no law to which appeal could be made, because all range users had equal privileges. Thus there was frequent resort to strong-arm methods to prevent the intrusion of sheep on what the cattlemen regarded as their own rightful grazing lands. Another factor was competition for use of the range between small and large livestock owners. Small owners sometimes found their stock crowded off the range by large owners, and frequently the existence of monopolies of large areas of public forest land by a few companies became matters of common complaint.

By 1906 considerable progress had been made toward a reconciliation of the conflicting interests of livestock owners on public forest land. Most owners began to see that grazing control by the Forest Service brought law and order to forest ranges in place of virtual civil war. At the same time Pinchot was becoming increasingly convinced that the government should charge a grazing fee to help pay the cost of providing grazing control. After the Chief Forester failed in efforts to get specific Congressional authority to impose grazing fees he carried his case to President Roosevelt who unhesitatingly supported it and obtained a favorable legal opinion on it from his Attorney General. This opinion held that under the Act of June 4, 1897, relating to forest reserves a reasonable charge could be made for the use and occupation of the reserves whenever such a policy seemed consistent with their purposes and protection.[8] With this sanction the Forest Service in 1906 began to impose fees for grazing on the lands under its jurisdiction. These fees, it will be shown later, provoked much criticism of the Forest Service and opposition to Pinchot's conservation efforts.

Since those who used national forest timber and grazing resources for commercial profit were required to pay a reasonable charge, the Chief Forester held that all persons or corporations who used the forest resources for commercial profit should be required to pay a charge. Thus, late in 1905 the Forest Service began to impose a fee for the use of national forest land for waterpower development purposes. This

---

[8] Attorney General Moody to Secretary Wilson, May 31, 1905, Law Office Correspondence, RG 95.

policy assumed that the appropriation of water was subject to state laws, but the Forest Service, by maintaining the forest cover, furnished the regular flow of water instead of alternate floods and drought and provided the fall which made possible the production of waterpower. For these services and rights of way for pipe and transmission lines, power houses, and other facilities the Service might properly make a reasonable charge to permittees who were given the exclusive use of national forest land for commercial power purposes.[9] The policy behind the charge was also designed to prevent speculative acquisition of power sites or privilege of use without development, to protect public interests through provisions enabling possible effective regulation of rates, services, and financing methods, and especially to prevent inclusion in the rate base of unearned increment in land values or of inflated capitalization.[10]

Many industrial leaders opposed Pinchot's waterpower policy. They contended that the federal government should make a grant in perpetuity of the forest land needed for their companies on condition that a certain minimum of development work be done. It should make a charge differing on each watershed and measured by the fair share of the power companies in the costs of conservation in the forests. The Chief Forester, however, strongly opposed perpetual grants of natural resources and ardently championed the requirement of a reasonable charge for waterpower. He held that the experience of the country with regard to oil, coal, and other major necessities of industrial and community life was sufficient basis for the belief that waterpower would be controlled by a small number of large corporations and that government control should be exercised to prevent this. He admitted that the power companies had a real grievance in the regulation, under an act of Congress of February 5, 1901, that made their permits revocable at the discretion of the Secretary of Agriculture. This regulation, he urged, should be revised so that the issuance of permits might become irrevocable, except for breach of conditions, for a fixed term sufficiently long to insure security of investment.[11]

The question of the need for federal regulation of waterpower development involving the use of public land led to the broadening of the issue to include navigable streams. The authority of the federal gov-

[9] *Report of the Forester, 1906*, p. 11; Pinchot to Roosevelt, January 2, 1907; Pinchot to H. J. Holmes, March 30, 1907, Law Office Correspondence, RG 95.

[10] Darrell H. Smith, *Forest Service*, p. 47.

[11] Pinchot to Roosevelt, January 2, 1907, Law Office Correspondence, RG 95.

ernment to impose conditions designed to safeguard and promote their navigability was fully established and was being used. There was a question, however, as to whether this authority extended far enough to afford a basis for applying a regulatory policy similar to that applied through federal land ownership. Pinchot and other conservationists held that there was such authority. Opponents tried to prevent the application of such a policy on the ground that it would violate private property and states' rights and was unnecessary.

Special Congressional authority and approval of construction plans by the War Department had to be obtained in order to construct a dam affecting navigation. Under the general dam act of June 21, 1906 (34 Stat. L. 386), the War Department was empowered to impose such conditions as it might consider necessary "to protect the present and future interests of the United States." Thus arose the question whether under this authorization a charge could be imposed and a time limitation set — the two points at issue in the early contest for regulation. In vetoing the Rainy River bill in 1908 President Roosevelt asserted:

> All grounds for such doubt should be removed henceforth by the insertion in every act granting such a permit of words adequate to show that a time limit and a charge to be paid to the government are among the interests of the United States which should be protected through conditions and stipulations. . . . I do not believe that natural resources should be granted and held in an undeveloped condition either for speculative or other reasons. . . . In place of the present haphazard policy of permanently alienating valuable public property we should substitute a definite policy.[12]

Requisite in such a policy were specified a limited time within which plans must be developed and the project executed, provision for annulling the grant if the conditions were not met, provision to insure full development of the navigation and power, a fee so adjustable in the future as to secure control in the public interest, and a fixed time limit on the duration of the grant. These stipulations for power development affecting the navigability of streams thus constituted a policy quite similar to Pinchot's with regard to such development on national forest land. This issue of the federal regulation of waterpower development was not to be fully settled until the passage of the Federal Power Act of June 10, 1920 adopting the principle of public regula-

---

[12] 60th Congress, 1st Sess., *Congressional Record*, pp. 4698–4699.

tion of hydroelectric power long advocated by the founder of the national forest system.[13]

The creation of a national forest on the public domain withdrew land from the operation of the Homestead Act. However, tracts suitable for agricultural use were often to be found within a forest. Pinchot favored a measure enacted by Congress on June 11, 1906, which provided that on application from anyone an examination should be made of lands thought to be more suitable for agriculture than for growing timber. If such proved to be the case, these areas were to be opened to homestead entry. His approval of this measure was consistent with his policy of conservative forest use. Under this law, which became known as the Forest Homestead Act of 1906, an examination was made to determine whether the land was capable of producing crops, and in deciding this the soil, climate, altitude, and slope were taken into consideration. Lands valuable for grazing only were not listed under the law. By 1910 the total area listed for homesteads comprised 628,872 acres.[14]

Early in his career as a forester, Pinchot had recognized that the value of forests for timber, grazing, and other purposes depended directly upon their protection from fire. He knew that conflagrations were the most destructive sources of devastation of American forests, despite the dearth of historical and scientific data concerning the causes and extent of such damage. Consequently, in federal forestry, the study of forest fires became one of his first programs. Much valuable information was obtained from the study for use in arousing popular sentiment for more adequate fire laws, and to aid investigations in forest management.[15]

When control of the national forests passed to the Bureau of Forestry, as the Forest Service was still called in 1905, Pinchot and his force put into practice the knowledge gained from their earlier studies of forest fires. They made substantial progress in reducing damage to the forests and in developing fire patrol and fighting methods. During 1905, fire burned over an area of 279,592 acres in the national forests. In 1906 the area burned over was 115,416 acres and in 1907 only 194,101 acres,[16] despite the fact that the total national forest area

[13] 41 Stat. L., 1063; Editorial in the *Journal of Forestry*, XLIII (August 1945), 548; Hays, *Conservation and the Gospel of Efficiency*, p. 81.

[14] U.S.D.A., *Annual Reports*, 1910, pp. 366–369.

[15] *Report of the Forester, 1904*, p. 26.

[16] Paper titled, "Special Data on National Forest Policy," 1908, Division of Operations Correspondence, RG 95.

was steadily expanding during these years. According to the Committee on Forestry of the Denver Chamber of Commerce and Board of Trade, if the sole duty of the federal forest rangers had been limited to patrolling national forests for the purpose of preventing and extinguishing fires in their incipiency, the amount saved from year to year would have covered many times the cost of such service. The Committee also commended the rangers for their efficiency in taking charge of fires on State and private lands.[17] Notwithstanding this advance in prevention, fires from locomotives, lightning, carelessness in burning slashings, and incendiarism still continued to be the greatest of forest evils during and after Pinchot's administration.

[17] Report of the Committee on Forestry of the Denver Chamber of Commerce and Board of Trade, January 27, 1909, General Correspondence, RG 95.

IX

Chief Forester and the Forest Service

M UCH OF Pinchot's success in the fight for the conservation of forests and other natural resources was due to the efficient and loyal support of the Forest Service. This organization, which he created and inspired, was widely considered as the model in administrative efficiency and *esprit de corps* of the entire Federal Government.[1] Heading the Service as the Chief Forester with the modest salary of $3,500, increased to $5,000 in 1907, Pinchot surrounded himself with capable men and threw his tremendous energy into the development of the Service. Basic in his organization methods was the principle of individual recognition and responsibility. As he saw it, the first step in setting up a project "was to find the right man and see that he understood the scope and limits of his work and just what was expected of him" and "the next step was to give him his head and let him use it." An executive official in charge of particular work should be held responsible for results, but should also be given the outward signs of his responsibility, including, for example, the right to sign letters relating specifically to his own work. In short, the right man should have a chance to do his work and the means to do it. More important still, he should be given full credit for good work that he might accomplish.[2]

---

[1] See McGeary, *Gifford Pinchot*, pp. 91–94.
[2] *Breaking New Ground*, p. 282.

The Forester stoutly insisted that his organization was no place for known incompetent employees or political appointees. His boast that "no man who failed was kicked upstairs, and no failure held a job in the Forest Service" was extravagant, but it represented an ideal to be attained.[3] Estimating that the value of public services by political appointees runs from "exactly zero . . . to from 50 to 75 per cent of the same services by honestly chosen civil service appointees," he adhered to civil service rules in making appointments. Moreover, political activities of Forest Service employees were frowned upon. A forest officer was considered to have the right to act upon his political convictions as was any other citizen, but he was not expected to allow them to interfere with his work.[4] These were fundamental considerations in the Forester's administrative practices.

From the very beginning Pinchot aimed to bring the administration of the reserves near to the people whose wants they served and to transact business quickly without neglecting necessary safeguards. Thus he gave considerable executive authority to local Forest Service officials and endeavored to keep the field work at a high standard by making frequent field inspections himself and maintaining a staff of inspectors who reported to him.[5] The heads of branches into which the Service was divided — each in his own line, such as grazing, timber-management, extension — directed work on the ground through forest supervisors. Under the supervisors were the rangers with whom ordinary forest users did most of their business.

In order to expedite and render more effective and economical the work of administering the national forests, Pinchot in 1908 established field headquarters in six districts in which the forests were grouped. These headquarters were located in Missoula, Montana; Denver, Colorado; Albuquerque, New Mexico; Salt Lake City, Utah; San Francisco, California; and Portland, Oregon. Under this reorganization a forester in charge of each district dealt directly with the supervisors of the forests of his district. Only questions of special importance were to be submitted to the central office in Washington. In this way, it was hoped that the regular business of the forests would be expedited and the men in charge of the business would be in close touch with the users of the forests. In addition, modeling the district offices after the

---

[3] *Breaking New Ground*, p. 283.
[4] Pinchot to Governor F. R. Gooding of Idaho, November 23, 1906, General Correspondence, RG 95.
[5] *Report of the Forester*, 1905, p. 2.

Washington office, Pinchot put specialists in charge of silviculture, grazing, operations, and other lines of field work.[6] This form of decentralized organization has remained basically unchanged from Pinchot's administration to the present.[7] It appears to have been immediately successful in producing greater dispatch of business, closer contact between office and field, and more efficiency along all lines of work. As early as 1909 Secretary of Agriculture Wilson lauded the change as the "most important step ever taken by the Forest Service — taking the Department to the people."[8] The district system of localized forest administration permitting field men to make on-the-ground decisions has often been judged a vital factor in facilitating effective national-forest management.[9]

Under this system Pinchot eventually administered nearly 200,000,000 acres of forest land — an area equal to all of New England and most of the Middle Atlantic States, a domain greater than the German Empire. The American Forestry Association estimated that the total economic value of the forests was over $14,000,000,000. This included the value of the stumpage and of the land as a timber producer, grazing area for livestock, conservator of water for irrigation and industrial power, and for other purposes. Included also was the value of permanent improvements then on the reserves. Stated another way, the Forester was considered to have under his control property which exceeded in value all the forts, arsenals, navy yards, and warships of the United States.[10] The administration of such valuable resources was a great responsibility touching many vital interests. Little wonder, then, that some Americans considered Pinchot a great public servant while others called him a bureaucratic tyrant.

Next in authority to Chief Forester Pinchot as administrator of this vast public estate was the Associate Forester, Overton W. Price, who had been appointed a special agent in the old Division of Forestry in May 1899 and had risen rapidly through the positions of field assistant, superintendent of working plans, and assistant forester. His two years of forestry training in Germany and Switzerland gave him a more thorough technical background than that of his Chief. Loyal, courageous, and endowed with remarkable executive capacity, he was the

[6] Press releases on the field headquarters for the Forest Service, 1908, RG 95.
[7] Earl W. Loveridge, "The Administration of National Forests," *Trees. The Yearbook of Agriculture, 1949* (U.S.D.A., Washington, 1949), p. 373.
[8] U.S.D.A., *Annual Reports, 1909*, p. 95.
[9] Loveridge, pp. 373–379.
[10] Boston (Massachusetts) *Transcript*, April 13, 1907.

principal architect of the inner organizational structure of the Forest Service and the chief engineer of its intricate administrative operations. Thanks to his loyalty and ability, Pinchot was able to leave the management of the Service in his hands while he served on a half a dozen presidential commissions during his tenure as Federal Forester. It is not surprising that he considered Price "one of the most effective and useful men" whom he had ever met in the government service.[11]

Yale classmate, friend, and right-hand adviser of the Chief Forester in early legal matters of the Service was George W. Woodruff. Before the transfer of the forest reserves to Pinchot's control he carefully studied legislation relating to the public domain, kept supporters of forestry in Congress posted on pending bills, and furnished them with facts and arguments that they needed to defend forestry proposals. Physically robust and mentally brilliant and energetic during critical periods, he often devoted thirteen hours daily to the legal affairs of the Service. His interpretations of forestry law were sustained on the eleven occasions that they were carried to the Supreme Court of the United States. President Roosevelt credited him with a significant contribution to American political theory when he declared: "The idea that the Executive is the steward of the public welfare was first formulated and given practical effect in the Forest Service by its law officer, George Woodruff."

When Woodruff became Assistant Attorney General for the Interior Department in March 1907, Philip P. Wells, Yale Law School instructor and former classmate of Pinchot, took over the legal work of the Forest Service. The Forester considered Woodruff to be "the first authority in America on the law of Conservation" and held that Wells "was without a rival in his legal knowledge of water power and utilities in general." He was proud to have had both of them in his bureau and later, as Governor of Pennsylvania, he was happy to have them as his principal legal advisers.[12]

Herbert A. Smith, editor of Forest Service publications and director of publicity, was another intimate and valued adviser. It was he who drafted the Forester's annual reports to the Secretary of Agriculture, passages on forestry in the Secretary's annual reports to the President, and many writings and speeches on forestry and conservation of Pinchot, the President, and other public figures. He was considered the

---

[11] Pinchot to Secretary Wilson, December 30, 1905, RG 95.
[12] *Breaking New Ground*, pp. 302–304.

nation's most able authority on the history of American forestry. Well did he serve Pinchot and many Service Chiefs that followed him.[13]

Many other persons also helped the Service to attain its reputation for efficiency and high morale. George B. Sudworth, highly trained in the botanical knowledge of trees, conducted pioneer studies relating to the history and description of forest resources. Raphael Zon, early advocate of forest research and studies of the economic utilization of forest products, laid before Pinchot the plan which culminated in the establishment of Service experiment stations to study the best possible management of the forest and the range. Other able and devoted officials in the headquarters office in Washington were William L. Hall, James B. Adams, William T. Cox, Albert F. Potter, and Royal S. Kellogg. In the field organization were William B. Greeley, Robert Y. Stuart, Ferdinand A. Silcox, and Earle H. Clapp, all of whom later served as head of the Service.

The spirit and enthusiasm that animated personnel of the Forest Service during its early years was a favorite theme of newspaper writers. Most of them were much impressed by the youthfulness of the officials and described the headquarters office as a veritable beehive of activity. The following impression was typical:

> There's something characteristic in the head men of the forest service as if they had been inoculated with the Roosevelt-Pinchot virus; they are enthusiasts, every one of them. They give the impression that they are working for love of the forests — nature lovers bent on a great cause. Mr. Pinchot has enthusiasm to a degree, but more than that he can spread the contagion. In this respect the service is distinct. It keeps free from taint of bureaucracy in its dealings with the public. The people are taken into the confidence of the chiefs. And too there is the 'tang' of the woods about most of them as if they were fit to do their century on a moment's notice or climb a Colorado peak for the love of the thing.[14]

High morale was not confined to the Washington office of the Service. It obtained also in the field. Important here was Pinchot's reputation for providing full support to his officials in the performance of their duties. One of them later declared: "I know how much it meant to the young foresters who were put in charge of national forests in a sheep or cattle country, where through a misunderstanding of what it

---

[13] *Breaking New Ground*, pp. 304–305.
[14] Denver (Colorado) *Republican*, April 29, 1909.

was all about no foresters were then welcome, to be sure that they had the unquestioned backing of their superiors; that behind them was Gifford Pinchot, and that, if necessary, behind him was Theodore Roosevelt and the United States Army."[15]

With journalists, a subject still more popular was the Forester himself, who stirred subordinates to such great enthusiasm. Almost invariably they described him as a fighter, crusader, or a revolutionary example of the public official genus. Still a bachelor at forty, possessing a comfortable income independent of his government salary, and preferring hard, grinding work to leisure, Pinchot naturally evoked curiosity. He was frequently depicted at work in his new office in the Atlantic Building on F Street in downtown Washington. Nearly always the picture was of a busy man seated at a plain desk with a pile of papers before him, scanning sheet after sheet of typewritten manuscript. It was the story of an executive seemingly possessed of a demon of work but never too busy to confer with a subordinate official on a problem, or consider a complaint by a forest user.

Even more dynamic and inspiring was Pinchot when he made inspection trips in the field. Such trips were made as often as his duties in Washington would permit. Frequently he would say to a friend: "I am getting too much office work for the good of my soul. I must get out into the field."[16] It was a highlight in the experience of a forest supervisor to accompany the energetic Forester on an inspection trip. William B. Greeley, a forest supervisor who later became head of the Service, has vividly described such an occasion:

> I got to know G. P. as men can know each other only in camp and on the trail. We worked timber together on one of the sales areas; we scaled a couple of peaks where fire lookouts were planned; we met rangers and cowmen and prospectors. . . . He could outride and outshoot any ranger on the force. . . . He told us of his plans for the Service and the next moves in the national march of conservation. He made us . . . feel like soldiers in a patriotic cause.[17]

Such was the inspiration that "G. P." gave to his force — a devoted working army of 2,500 men. One would have to look far indeed in

[15] Ralph S. Hosmer, "Some Recollections of Gifford Pinchot, 1898–1904," *Journal of Forestry*, XLIII (August 1945), 558–562.
[16] Pinchot to Dr. Alexander Lambert, November 23, 1905, Office of Forest Reserves Correspondence, RG 95.
[17] William B. Greeley, *Forests and Men* (New York, 1951), pp. 81–82.

government service or private enterprise to find the counterpart of such inspired leadership.

By 1907, investigators of government organization and methods had begun to consider the Forest Service one of the best organized and most businesslike federal agencies. Senator Beveridge (Indiana) and others indicated that the President desired it to serve as the example and inspiration for reform in methods throughout the federal government.[18] Even more signal praise came in 1908, when the firm of Gunn, Richards and Company of New York City, consultants in business organization and methods, reporting on their investigation of the Forest Service, stated:

> We can not praise too highly the personnel of the Service, and we have much pleasure in stating that, in our rather extended experience in commercial enterprises where the opportunity for financial reward is unlimited, we have rarely, if ever, met a body of men where the average of intelligence was so high or the loyalty to the organization and to the work so great. Without exception, every individual with whom we came in contact was most enthusiastic in regard to the work, and anxious to promote the welfare of the Service in every manner possible.
>
> The volume of the business transacted, in our opinion, compares most favorably with that in commercial practice and is worthy of the highest commendation.[19]

While the evidence of efficiency and high morale under Pinchot's administration is almost overwhelming, there is no reason to assume that everything was entirely sweetness and light in his official family. Not all Forest Service employees were able to live up to his high work standards. There were some complaints that he never seemed to forget a man's mistakes or failures, and tended to deny to one who had stumbled an opportunity to make good. According to F. E. Olmsted, whom Pinchot considered one of his most competent field officials, this impression sometimes engendered a hopeless attitude and "caused a feeling of serious uncertainty about the permanency, desirability, and pleasure of work in the Service."[20]

---

[18] Washington (D.C.) *Post*, March 31, 1907; *National Tribune* (D.C.), September 28, 1907; *Report of the Committee on Expenditures in the Department of Agriculture* (House Report No. 8147, 59th Congress, 2d Sess., 1907), p. 18.

[19] Report of Gunn, Richards and Company, June 30, 1908, pp. 1–2, Research Compilation File, RG 95.

[20] F. E. Olmsted to O. W. Price, August 17, 1908, Section of Inspection Correspondence, RG 95.

The Forester's passion for administrative efficiency sometimes led him to advocate extreme measures and to express opinions that were probably unpopular with many of his bureau employees. To prevent delay in answering departmental correspondence he once asked Associate Forester Price what he would think of the idea of having office desk drawers nailed up so that officials of the Service could not put away letters requiring replies.[21] Price apparently persuaded him not to issue such a drastic order. Another incident illustrates Pinchot's passion for getting work done promptly and efficiently. To a request for an opinion on a bill to shorten by one-half hour the daily working hours of federal government employees, he replied that he "would be particularly sorry to see the hours of labor shortened, since the existing schedule of seven hours enabled the Forest Service to accomplish correspondingly more work with the same force, without loss in efficiency and without the infliction of any hardship whatever upon the employees." Furthermore, he thought that, compared with the working hours required in private business, those in federal government agencies were "exceedingly moderate."[22]

Ill will against the Forest Service was created occasionally by some forest officials who were unduly aggressive in enforcing forest regulations against the interests of local residents, or who were anxious to assert federal authority over local authority and practices. In an incident of this nature the Chief Forester had to warn a field official: "In Government work the soft pedal is essential. 'Step softly and carry a big stick.' But don't use the stick. It is especially important that irregular methods, such as you used in several cases, and quarrels with local residents should be avoided."[23]

In attempting to justify their officious acts, field men sometimes ignored their immediate supervisors and appealed their case directly to the Chief Forester in Washington. In such instances field supervisors rightly felt that their authority was being undermined. In addition, forest officials in their anxiety to do everything possible to extend the national forest system were often accused of engaging in local politics. For example, Governor F. R. Gooding of Idaho, who opposed the creation of additional national forests in his state, complained that in his campaign for reelection in 1906 the Federal forest rangers and

---

[21] Pinchot to Price, September 8, 1905, General Correspondence, RG 95.
[22] Pinchot to Secretary Wilson, February 15, 1906, General Correspondence, RG 95.
[23] Pinchot to S. M. Cross, August 10, 1908, General Correspondence, RG 95.

supervisors in the state neglected their duties to engage in political activities against him.[24]

There is considerable reason to conclude that the administrative difficulties and mistakes of the Forest Service stemmed mainly from the attempt to bring about too many changes all at once, rather than from fundamental deficiencies in organization or from improper administrative methods. It attempted to change quickly long-established concepts of the use of forest resources. It moved rapidly to halt practices on timberlands and the range that had long been considered legitimate and even essential to national development. It resorted to some methods not equally applicable to all economic conditions throughout a rapidly expanding national forest system.

---

[24] Governor Gooding to Pinchot, November 15, 1908, Office of Organization Correspondence, RG 95.

X

Pinchotism

A<small>LTHOUGH</small> Pinchot's policies and methods for the protection and conservation use of forests steadily gained national support during Theodore Roosevelt's administration, they were being vigorously criticized by certain groups and individuals, especially in western sections of the United States. These critics directed their hostility against what they called "Pinchotism," which became a term for all that they considered arbitrary, undesirable, unreasonable, and even un-American in the administration of the national forest system. Fundamentally, their criticism stemmed from traditional pioneer individualism, the desire to exploit the country's resources unhampered by government restriction. Their target was the Forester, both as a person and as an administrator of great authority.

To begin with, the fact that Pinchot was an eastern man, wealthy, and represented by some as an aristocrat, did not raise him in the estimation of western residents. To many of this group he also seemed, or was represented to be, an impractical theorist with grandiose plans for the building of a great federal empire in sovereign states of the West, or for the treatment of them as a detached suburb of Washington, D.C. The eventual acerbity with which the cry of Pinchotism was raised by some westerners was illustrated in the remark of a miner: "Cecil Rhodes was not within 1,000,000 miles of exerting the power that Gifford the First claimed to himself. This enormous territory of Forest reserves is an empire within a republic, ruled by a despot with as much power as the Czar of Russia."[1] Newspapers in Colorado frequently depicted the Forester as a veritable despot. The *Rocky Mountain News* once carried a cartoon of him titled "Czar Pinchot and His Cossack Rangers Administering the Forest Reserves." In it he was pictured as a czar seated on a throne, and flanked by a Cossack-like ranger, with a miner, pioneer, and settler kneeling before him.[2] Less severe critics made much of the independent way in which Pinchot seemed to exercise his authority, since officially he was only a bureau chief under the Secretary of Agriculture. Thus a western newspaper reporter observed: "Few people realized there was any one in authority over Pinchot except the president and no one, apparently, was less conscious of the fact than Pinchot himself. He went about the affairs of the forest service as if he were in independent command . . . and out West, especially, they got the notion that Pinchot was about the biggest thing in Washington."[3]

Pinchotism was also a rallying cry for many who opposed the extension of the national forest system. Against this extension many arguments were marshaled. Prominent was the contention that national forests tended to restrict mining and agriculture, since they caused large areas of the public domain to be withdrawn from settlement and unregulated use. Timber sales on them, it was said, promoted competition with private lumbering. The forests obstructed the building of hydraulic plants for generating cheaper power and light for industrial and domestic purposes. They caused large portions of land to be withheld from state taxation and fees for their use imposed burdens on the development of natural resources. It was even argued that the national forest system drove home-seekers to other countries and was nothing less than "an unwelcome importation" and a "miserable misfit amongst our free American institutions."[4]

Furthermore, many who professed to believe in a policy of conservative use of public forests and who conceded in theory the value of the national forest system still raised objections to Pinchot's administration of the system. They too spoke glibly of Pinchotism. In this group

[1] Speech of F. H. Stannard at the American Mining Congress at Seattle, Spokane (Washington) *Chronicle*, November 27, 1912.

[2] *Rocky Mountain News*, Denver, Colorado, September 16, 1908.

[3] Pueblo (Colorado) *Star Journal*, April 20, 1909.

[4] These views were forcefully presented by State Senator Elias M. Ammons in a speech before the Colorado General Assembly in April 1909. See the *Congressional Record*, Vol. 45, part 6, p. 6526 (61st Congress, 2d Sess., May 19, 1910).

were spokesmen of mining interests who charged that the Forester administered a commercial policy which directly increased the cost of mining and involved the industry in compliance with time-consuming official regulations which indirectly increased further the cost of mining. These added costs and official regulations were said to have been specifically waived or disclaimed as governmental policy in the mining statutes of the United States and thus the costs and regulations imposed by the Forest Service conflicted with this earlier governmental policy provided by the mining statutes.[5] Likewise, representatives of the National Wool Growers Association accused the Service of imposing burdensome fines, without a hearing, upon grazers under the pretext of demands for damages consequent upon a violation of Service regulations or for trespass, accompanied with the threat that in default of payment within a brief period, the grazing permit of the alleged offender would be canceled and his stock driven off the forest. They also complained that charges for sheep grazing were excessive as compared to those for cattle.[6] Others voiced criticisms of administrative delays in issuing grazing permits and in the examination of lands applied for, for agricultural settlement, under the Forest Homestead Act of June 11, 1906, and charges that the timber sales policy favored large corporations rather than small consumers and tended to strip the West of its timber supplies. Judge D. C. Beaman of Denver, Colorado, a prominent critic of Pinchot, thought that the complaints of the people were not so much because forest employees obstructed the homesteader, miner, and stockman as because the rules governing forests compelled them to do so. "Mr. Pinchot," said he, "is the chief offender."[7]

Anti-Pinchot feeling had come to a head in connection with the debate on the Agricultural Appropriation Bill of 1907. The debate was precipitated by an amendment to the bill inserted by the House Committee on Agriculture which would permit the Secretary of Agriculture (through the Forest Service) to divide the national forests into such administrative units as he might deem wise. Representatives Tawney of Minnesota, and Mondell of Wyoming led a vigorous but unsuccessful opposition to the bill in the House. Opponents of the bill and the Forest Service were more successful in the Senate where the attack

[5] *The Mining World*, Chicago, November 6, 1908.
[6] Resolutions of the National Wool Growers Association, January 20, 1908, Division of Range Management Correspondence, RG 95.
[7] *The Irrigation Age*, November 1908.

was led by Senators Fulton of Oregon, Patterson of Colorado, and
Carter of Montana. In one of the most scathing denunciations ever
heard in the Senate, Fulton declared:

> The truth is this Bureau (the Forest Service) is composed of
> dreamers and theorists, but beyond and outside the domain of
> their theories and their dreams is the everyday, busy, bustling,
> throbbing world of human endeavor where real men are at work
> producing substantial results. . . . While these chiefs of the
> Bureau of Forestry sit within their marble halls and theorize and
> dream of waters conserved, forests and streams protected and
> preserved throughout the ages and the ages, the lowly pioneer
> is climbing the mountain side where he will erect his humble
> cabin, and within the shadow of the whispering pines and the
> lofty firs of the forest engage in the laborious work of carving
> out for himself and his loved ones a home and a dwelling place.[8]

In this debate Secretary of the Interior Ethan Allen Hitchcock was
also criticized for abuses under the Forest Lieu Act. The national forests were defended by Senators from all sections of the country. Especially outstanding in this defense were Senators Dolliver of Iowa,
Beveridge of Indiana, Spooner of Wisconsin, Proctor of Vermont, Newlands of Nevada, Dubois of Idaho, and Perkins and Flint of California.

After several days of debate the anti-forestry group won some success with the enactment of an amendment to the Agricultural Appropriation Bill which provided that "hereafter no forest reserve shall be
created, nor shall any addition be made to one heretofore created,
within the limits of the states of Oregon, Washington, Idaho, Montana, Colorado, or Wyoming, except by an act of Congress."[9] This
amendment signified the repeal of the forestry act of 1891, which had
enabled the President to create forest reserves, and in view of strong
Congressional hostility indicated that probably few, if any, more reserves, would be established in those specified six states of the North-
west which contained the great bulk of western timber. Much of the
force of the amendment was taken away, however, by President Roosevelt when on March 2, 1907, before signing the appropriation bill, he
proclaimed, mainly with Pinchot's advice, twenty-one new national
forests in the six states.

Critics of national forest policy also won other concessions in the

---

[8] *Congressional Record*, February 18, 1907, p. 3188.
[9] *Congressional Record*, February 23, 1907, p. 3722.

Agricultural Appropriation Bill of 1907. The forest reserve special fund, by which, since 1905, receipts from the sale of timber and grazing privileges had been available for Forest Service work, was now abolished. It was also provided that 10 per cent of the receipts of each national forest should be given to the state for schools and roads in the counties where the forest was situated. Finally the Secretary of Agriculture was required to submit to Congress each year a detailed report of all receipts from national forest administration.

To the various criticisms made of him Pinchot steadfastly held that his administrative policies and methods for the conservative use of national forest resources were legal and justified by the public interest. He expected assaults "from self-seeking interests, as well as from short-sighted persons" who were "unable to distinguish between an immediate small advantage and a great permanent good."[10] Insisting that there was some opposition to the administration of national forests which could not and ought not to be removed, he felt that, if there were no opposition, it would be the clearest possible indication that such administration was not performing its public duty. In the exercise of the duty imposed upon it, he contended that the service frequently prevented certain men or interests from getting things that they desired, but ought not to have. From these men and interests had come the bitterest and most persistent opposition. Such interests were represented, for example, by some of the wealthy sheep men, who objected to making room for the small settler, or to such reduction in the number of their stock as was necessary to protect irrigation interests, and by men who were engaged in the formation of a great water-power trust. For the opposition he had aroused from selfish interests he had no apologies to make. He proposed to stand resolutely by a policy of preferring to help the "small man" make a living from forest resources rather than one of helping the "large man" make a profit. If his position in these matters led to irritation and denunciation, then let his opponents make the most of it. In fundamental policies for conservative forest use there would be no "backward step."[11]

In the great amount of business transacted over so large an area as the national forests embraced, Pinchot conceded that some mistakes had been made and some injustice done in isolated cases. Whenever such mistakes or injustice had been brought to his attention, he

[10] *Report of the Forester, 1905*, p. 2.
[11] Speech of Pinchot at a session of the Colorado State Legislature on March 16, 1909, Denver *News*, March 17, 1909.

declared that steps had been taken to correct them. These were insignificant in amount and importance as compared to the good accomplished. Injustice had to be avoided as much to the government as to the users of national forests. If dishonest men did not attempt to make illegal use of public forest resources, there would be no need of government forest regulations.

His defense of Forest Service regulations issued without specific statutory authority, as in the case of grazing and water power fees, was based upon broad constitutional interpretation of executive and national authority. Pinchot pointed out that Congress had given to the Secretary of Agriculture, acting through the Forest Service, the specific task of administering the national forests, with full power of performance, and had given him authority to make such rules and regulations and establish such service as would insure the purposes of such forests; namely, to regulate their occupancy and use and to preserve them from destruction. The grazing, waterpower, and other regulations issued under the Congressional authority, he argued, were in accordance with principles laid down by the United States Supreme Court when in the case of McCulloch vs. Maryland (4 Wheat., 421) it ruled: "Let the end be legitimate, let it be within the scope of the Constitution, and all means which are appropriate, which are plainly adapted to that end, which are not prohibited, but consist with the letter and spirit of the Constitution, are constitutional." Pinchot could truthfully assert in 1910 that the Forest Service had not been defeated or reversed on any vital principle underlying its work in any court or administrative tribunal of last resort.

Summarizing his creed as a public servant he affirmed:

> It is the first duty of a public officer to obey the law. But it is his second duty, and a close second, to do everything the law will let him do for the public good, and not merely what the law directs or compels him to do. Unless the public service is alive enough to serve the people with enthusiasm, there is very little to be said for it.[12]

---

[12] Gifford Pinchot, *The Fight for Conservation* (New York, 1910), p. 117.

XI

Publicist and Educator

IN ADVANCE of other public officials of his day, Pinchot clearly understood how closely interrelated were propaganda, control of public opinion, political lobbies, law-making, and appropriations.[1] Hence, as head of the Forest Service he conducted an extensive and varied publicity program designed to acquaint the populace with the need for forest conservation and development and, thereby, to enlist support of the Service by the American people and their representatives in Congress. This program included the furnishing of technical information to individuals, on the ground or by correspondence; preparation and distribution of publications; public addresses; loan and sale of lantern slides, pictures, and other illustrative material for the use of lecturers, writers, and other persons; cooperation with teachers and public school officials in educational work; exhibits at expositions; and preparation of official information concerning forestry in brief statements given to newspapers and magazines for publication.

Unique and especially significant were methods used in the preparation and distribution of publications and news releases. Not only did the Chief Forester and most of his subordinate officials and technical experts do much writing for publication in official bulletins and in newspapers and magazines, but the Service also employed a few persons, usually experienced in newspaper work, primarily to edit manu-

---

[1] See Alpheus T. Mason, *Bureaucracy Convicts Itself. The Ballinger-Pinchot Controversy of 1910* (New York, 1941), p. 24; McGeary, *Gifford Pinchot*, pp. 88–90.

scripts for official publication and to distribute publications and news releases. Distribution of informational material was facilitated by the maintenance of a mailing list which by 1910 was said to contain 750,000 names.[2] The work of attending to this mailing list was apparently an expensive matter, since the installation of an addressing machine by the Service in 1908 was reported to have reduced the clerical force of the Service by thirty persons.

This work brought forth the charge that Pinchot was maintaining an expensive "press bureau" to influence public sentiment in favor of the Forest Service and to enhance his personal prestige. The *Irrigation Age* of Chicago called him "one of the best advertisers of himself and his work in the United States" and declared that he had Lydia Pinkham "beaten to a shade."[3] Perennial critics of Pinchot such as Senator Heyburn and Representative Mondell contended that not over 15 per cent of the annual appropriations for the Service were used directly in protection of the national forests but that a large share of the remainder of the appropriations had been spent for an unnecessarily large clerical force, traveling expenses for officials, unnecessary junkets, and the preparation of propaganda material to advertise the Service.

This so-called "press agent work" of the Forest Service was nonetheless considered to be very effective. It won admiration as well as denunciation because of the adroitness with which it successfully influenced public opinion and stimulated public action. The San Francisco *Bulletin* stated in 1908 that Pinchot with his "press agents" had built up such support for his bureau that he could obtain from Congress practically anything that he desired with regard to legislation and appropriations.[4] Even Secretary of Agriculture Wilson believed Congress felt that Pinchot's publicity efforts were being used "to set up a 'forest fire' behind them."[5]

Pinchot denied that his press work was for personal or bureau aggrandizement and contended that it constituted "the only defensible policy for any Government organization, any part of whose purpose is to collect and disseminate facts." Economy, promptness, and efficiency required that information gathered at public expense should be given

[2] Statement of Representative Frank Mondell, *Congressional Record*, February 1, 1910, p. 1359.
[3] *Irrigation Age*, June 1909.
[4] San Francisco *Bulletin*, December 24, 1908.
[5] Secretary Wilson to Pinchot, November 9, 1908, Letters Sent, RG 16.

to the people, who pay for it, as promptly, cheaply, and widely as possible.[6] The large population of the country could not be reached with a few thousand copies of government publications that "too often fall practically dead from the press," because their information is not presented in a manner interesting to the average reader. By employing men familiar with both the special requirements of newspaper work and the Forest Service, it became possible to carry on the work of popular education on a far more extensive scale, and at a far lower cost than in any other way. But above all, this publicity work was justified, the Chief Forester insisted, as a method of informing the people concerning the relation between the perpetuation of the forests and the public welfare. The character, intelligence, and news sense of the press were an effective barrier to any attempts of self-laudation by the Forest Service.[7] If the people were to have an accurate view of the existing conditions, they had to understand what was being done to help them, just as they should be informed of what was being done to hurt them. Hence, his administration proceeded on the "theory that publicity is the essential and indispensable condition of clean and effective public service."[8] Such was the Forester's defense of the publicity methods of his bureau. John Ise, an authority on American forest policy, concluded that without these methods Pinchot could not have accomplished much of his program for forest conservation.[9]

Many newspaper editors commended Pinchot's publicity methods. The suggestion that he was in collusion with newspapers to advertise himself and the Service at great government expense was branded as "ridiculous" by the editor of the Spokane *Spokesman-Review*. He asserted that many informative articles emanating from the Forest Service had been given wide publicity in newspapers, without cost to the government, as matters of news and because of their value to the public.[10] The Grand Rapids *News* declared that it would be greatly to the profit of the people of the United States if all government agencies "took as great pains to keep them informed" as the Forest Service was doing.[11] The *News* of Wheeling, West Virginia reasoned:

---

[6] Pinchot to Representative Ernest M. Pollard, April 1, 1908, Division of Operations Correspondence, RG 95.

[7] Pinchot to Representative Charles F. Scott, February 14, 1908, Division of Operations Correspondence, RG 95.

[8] 61st Congress, 3d Sess., Senate Doc. No. 719, IX, 5310–5311.

[9] John Ise, *The United States Forest Policy* (New Haven, 1924), p. 288.

[10] Spokane *Spokesman-Review*, April 1, 1908.

[11] Grand Rapids (Michigan) *News*, March 31, 1908.

It may be wrong to use government money for the purpose of informing the governed as to what their officials are doing, but the *News* is inclined to the opinion that the money Mr. Pinchot spends in this way is put to better use than the sums spent by congressmen in mailing broadcast copies of speeches they never made, the expense of printing and mailing being borne by the government.[12]

The belief of many Congressmen that the Forest Service was using Government money to prepare or, at least, suggest or skeletonize articles for publication criticizing unfriendly Congressmen or other public officials led in 1908 to the adoption of an amendment to the Agricultural Appropriation Bill which provided that no part of this appropriation should "be paid or used for the purpose of paying for in whole or in part the preparation or publication of any newspaper or magazine articles." It added, however, that this should not "prevent the giving out to all persons without discrimination, including newspaper and magazine writers and publishers, of facts or official information of value to the public."[13] The Forest Service stated this amendment was entirely satisfactory since it expressly sanctioned the work that it had been doing, that is, the dissemination of official information. The Service acknowledged that for several years it had prepared press bulletins, or short articles in newspaper form, concerning its work and forestry in general. Everyone who received this issuance knew where it came from and was free to use it either as official matter credited to the Service or without credit. The only way to prevent this, it contended, would be to pass a law providing a penalty for any newspaper which printed information which it received from the government without printing the fact that it was so received. This would be an absurdity. Writers of magazine and newspaper articles drew heavily upon the government for information, which, being public and gathered at public expense, should be made available to them for whatever purpose they desired to use it.[14]

Public addresses by Pinchot and other members of his staff constituted another important phase of Forest Service public relations. The Chief Forester attended and addressed as many meetings as possible to advance the cause of forestry and win support for the work of the Service. During 1907, for example, he attended officially or unofficially

---

[12] Wheeling (West Virginia) *News*, March 31, 1908.
[13] 35 Stat. L., 259. Similar provisions were inserted in later Agricultural Appropriation Acts.
[14] Press release of the U.S. Forest Service, August 5, 1908, RG 95.

President Theodore Roosevelt and Chief Forester Gifford Pinchot on the river steamer "Mississippi," during a trip of the Inland Waterways Commission in October 1907. (p. 108–109)

Gifford Pinchot, in 1908, at the time of his appointment as Chairman
of the National Conservation Commission.   (p. 111)

at least thirty-four meetings of such organizations as the American Forestry Association, National Wool Growers Association, American Livestock Association, United States Chamber of Commerce, National Drainage Congress, National Paper Trade Association, National Wholesale Lumber Dealers Association, and Association of Agricultural Colleges and Experiment Stations. Several addresses were also made before local commercial clubs and small groups of citizens.[15] Pinchot was not an orator but, rather, a straightforward, plain speaker. A listener once gave this description of him: "He talks quickly, and in jerky sentences that are yet connected. Like a fighting man, his face is lean and his eyes keen, though both have a softness and a quick responsiveness you don't find in the features of a man who is only a politician. In speaking, his arm crooks out from the elbow and his index finger admonishes his hearers as his hesitant quick sentences right truth in the homeliest of phrases."[16] The boldness and effectiveness of Pinchot's speeches was sometimes evidenced in the complaints of critics of his policies. In one instance Frank H. Short of Fresno, California, opposed to his ideas on waterpower regulation, remarked: "It has never before to my knowledge been true that an officer of an executive department of the Federal Government has found it compatible with his position or duties to go out in a public political capacity to discuss matters in this way and to laud those who agree with him and denounce those who oppose him."[17]

Officials of the Washington office and field offices of the Service were also encouraged and authorized to attend and address various public meetings. Occasionally, the Service hired special lecturers. One of them, E. A. Mills, was apparently very effective in helping to spread the doctrine of forest conservation. Mrs. Charles N. Jolls, vice-president of the Women's National Rivers and Harbors Congress, stated that if the Service had not sent Mills on a lecture trip in Delaware during 1907, a forestry bill would not have passed the state legislature two years later.[18] Mills was said to have been "remarkably successful" in his educational work, and the demand for his instruction in forest principles reportedly came from every part of the United States.[19] In con-

---

[15] 60th Congress, 1st Sess., Senate Doc. No. 485.
[16] Samuel W. Dibble in the Spokane *Spokesman-Review*, June 3, 1908.
[17] Short to Pinchot, September 15, 1909, Law Office Correspondence, RG 95.
[18] Mrs. Charles N. Jolls to Findley Burns, March 26, 1909, Information and Education Division Correspondence, RG 95.
[19] G. G. Anderson to Secretary Wilson, November 1, 1907, Information and Education Division Correspondence, RG 95.

trast, however, one of Pinchot's information assistants believed that the value of public addresses by members of the Forest Service was often overrated. He further declared: "Of the methods used by the Service to bring home to the people its work and aims and to disseminate information, the public address is the least effective and most costly. This is so chiefly because the speaker appeals to a comparatively insignificant audience." [20]

In any event, many Congressmen apparently felt that this lecture work was not only expensive but unnecessary and undesirable. In 1908 an amendment to the Agricultural Appropriation Act stipulated that none of the money appropriated should be used to pay traveling expenses of any forest official except on business directly connected with the Service. [21] Despite this, the Service was later accused of continuing to pay the expenses of officials who were merely lecturing at large to conventions and other meetings. Senator Heyburn, for example, as late as 1911 complained of the payment of such expenses of Service officials, who "stand before the national geographic societies and other learned societies with impressive titles and tell them how the world ought to be run." [22]

Another aspect of Pinchot's crusade to educate the public was his early effort to introduce forestry into the curriculum of schools and colleges. Foreseeing the need for professional education in forestry in the United States, he had persuaded his father and mother to join with him in establishing a school of forestry at Yale University. The school began in 1900 with an endowment from the Pinchot family of $150,000, which was later increased to $300,000. A summer session for the school's first-year students was opened on the Pinchot estate at Milford, Pennsylvania. In 1903 the Yale Corporation elected young Gifford to the position of professor of forestry in the Forest School. His duties included the presentation of a short course of lectures at New Haven each year and such assistance in the management of the School as he might give without conflict with his duties as Chief of the Bureau of Forestry in Washington. The Yale Forest School helped to supply men urgently needed in the task of inaugurating scientific forestry in the United States, and many leading officials of the Forest Service were its graduates. In unbroken succession from 1905 to 1940, the heads of

---

[20] Memorandum of Findley Burns on the lecture work of the Forest Service, March 9, 1909.
[21] 35 Stat. L., 259.
[22] Congressional Record, March 1, 1911, p. 3774.

the Service were founders or graduates of this professional institution. It was instrumental in establishing standards for American forestry education and supplying many teachers for new forest schools that soon sprang up all over the country.[23]

Professional standards in forestry were also advanced by the Society of American Foresters organized under Pinchot's leadership in November 1900. Associated with him in this effort were Henry S. Graves, Overton W. Price, Edward T. Allen, William L. Hall, Ralph S. Hosmer, and Thomas H. Sherrard, all Forestry Division employees who were destined to have important roles in Forest Service work and forestry education. These charter members of the Society announced their purpose: "To further the cause of forestry in America by fostering a spirit of comradeship among foresters; by creating opportunities for a free interchange of views upon forestry and allied subjects; and by disseminating a knowledge of the purpose and achievements of forestry." Pinchot was president of the Society during the periods 1900–08 and 1910–11 and was among the first group of distinguished Society members to be elected Fellows in 1918.[24] His Washington home was often the scene of informal meetings and suppers of the Society during its early years. Here on the evening of March 26, 1903, at Pinchot's invitation, President Roosevelt addressed the members in words to kindle enthusiasm and inspire zeal for the cause of forestry. From these beginnings the Society has grown into a vibrant organization that has achieved the purpose of its founders with conspicuous success. Its unity of fellowship is notable in public and private forest work and it has long been acknowledged as the principal spokesman of the profession of forestry in the United States and a leading force in the standardization of instruction in the nation's forest schools.

The fostering of cooperation between the Forest Service and educational institutions and societies was also important in the work of Pinchot as a publicist and educator. Working closely with the National Education Association, he maintained that the teaching of forestry was not only in the national interest as an aid to conservation, but also provided a means of training for industrial efficiency, especially in rural schools, and served as a pedagogic vehicle for illustrating the laws of evolution. "A piece of woodland which has not been altogether deprived of its natural character," he averred, "presents visibly before the

---

[23] *Breaking New Ground*, pp. 152–153.
[24] Ralph S. Hosmer, "The Society of American Foresters, An Historical Summary," *Journal of Forestry*, XLVIII (November 1950), 756–777.

eye not only the results but the actual working of the competitive struggle for existence and the survival of the fittest through adaptation to environment."[25]

By 1909 forestry was attracting wide attention in the schools of the United States. Not only were many colleges and universities introducing courses and even professional schools of forestry, but elementary phases of the subject were being introduced into hundreds of the elementary and secondary schools. Teachers gave enthusiastic reports of the success attending the new study. The public schools of Washington, D.C., and of parts of Iowa were in the vanguard of this movement. Every graded school in Washington and a large number of the rural schools of Pottawattamie County, Iowa, were then teaching the elements of forestry. In Iowa, the subject was taught as a commercial course in connection with local geography and agriculture, while in Washington it was used in the nature study courses. In the Forest Service, a section was devoted to cooperation with schools in teaching forestry and its related subjects. Technical schools of forestry as well as primary and even kindergarten public school grades could obtain the educational guidance of the Service; it was equally willing to help teach tree study to a nature class of first-graders and to assist in the establishment of a professional forest school. Most of the schools teaching forestry or related conservation topics used as textbooks several of the publications issued by the Forest Service, including Pinchot's famous *Primer of Forestry*.[26]

---

[25] Pinchot to Roosevelt, July 6, 1905, General Correspondence; Pinchot to Jean Dawson, October 16, 1905, Information and Education Division Correspondence, RG 95.
[26] Press release of the U.S. Forest Service, May 10, 1909, RG 95.

XII

Promoter of Forest Research

I N HIS TIRELESS CAMPAIGN to bring forestry out of the office and lecture hall and into the woods, Pinchot was alert to the need for more scientific knowledge of production characteristics and utilization potentialities of American forests. This realization was the stimulus to several efforts that laid the foundation for a broad program of forest research. In this connection were investigations in silviculture focusing directly on studies of commercially valuable trees. Pinchot's interest in such studies was evident as early as 1896 when he published *The White Pine* and two years later *The Adirondack Spruce*. His first annual report for the Division of Forestry noted that the prevailing ignorance of the rate of growth and habits of the country's principal timber trees made it "important to extend studies of them without delay." Listed as deserving immediate attention were surveys for such Eastern trees as the yellow poplar, black walnut, pencil cedar, and bald cypress, and Western ones such as the Douglas fir, lodge-pole pine, sugar pine, giant cedar, coast redwood, and yellow pine.[1]

From 1898 to 1905, these and other trees were scrutinized by Pinchot's forest assistants by means of field investigations in various parts of a particular tree's range of commercial distribution. Usually the required information concerned the tree's range; rate of growth; light, moisture, and soil requirements, reproduction, and behavior in pure stands and in competition with other species. Observations also often

---

[1] U.S.D.A., *Annual Reports*, 1898, p. 172.

dealt with the effect of lumbering upon reproduction and general market conditions for timber. Special attention was given to surveys for oak, yellow poplar, and hemlock in the Southern Appalacians; white and red pine in the Great Lakes states; western yellow pine and red fir in the North West; loblolly pine in Texas; and redwood, sugar pine, and eucalyptus in California. Facilitating these studies was the Section of Silvics, established by Pinchot in 1903 to coordinate and classify all data, gathered by the Bureau of Forestry or through other channels, that could "contribute to ordered and scientific knowledge" of American forests. The Section was also authorized to perform field work in silviculture. A wide spectrum of useful organized data was thus made available for men studying commercial trees.[2] These data were assembled in a little hall room of the Atlantic Building, which Pinchot, with some justification, called the "first cradle and treasure house of forest research in America."[3] These collected reference materials became the "Research Compilation" file — perhaps the most valuable body of forestry records now preserved in the National Archives.[4]

Numerous studies of forest conditions in particular states or regions were also providing useful silvicultural information. Conducted by Pinchot's agency in cooperation mainly with the U.S. Geological Survey and state forest organizations, the studies usually yielded data concerning the kind, quality, distribution, and stand of forest trees and the effects of lumbering, fire, grazing, climate, or other factors on forest growth. These joint programs received greatest attention prior to administration of federal forest lands by the Forest Service and dealt with a great variety of forest types in such states and territories as Maryland, Michigan, New Hampshire, Texas, California, Puerto Rico, and Hawaii. After 1905 the cooperative efforts were sometimes broadened to include economic considerations such as timber marketing and taxation of forest lands. Meanwhile, dendrological studies initiated by George B. Sudworth during Fernow's administration were continued by Pinchot. Noteworthy products of this work were several popular publications describing the distribution and silvical characteristics of tree species in the United States.

---

[2] U.S.D.A., *Annual Reports, 1904*, p. 176; Pinchot to Raphael G. Zon, July 17, 1903, General Correspondence, RG 95.

[3] *Breaking New Ground*, p. 308.

[4] See Harold T. Pinkett, "Records of Research Units of the United States Forest Service in the National Archives," *Journal of Forestry*, XLV (April 1947), 272–275.

The quest for scientific knowledge to facilitate forest management was also evident in tree planting experiments conducted prior to 1905 mainly on private lands and thereafter on national forest lands. In established sample plots, all trees were measured and various characteristics of their growth were noted. Trees on private lands apparently did not afford useful information, since the plots were not protected against destructive influences prior to the time of a second measurement. On government lands, however, despite frequent neglect due to a shortage of research men, the trees yielded better data.[5] By 1907 the Forest Service was also cooperating with several universities and state agricultural experiment stations in tree planting experiments designing to ascertain what species were best adapted to different regions; to improve methods of nursery planting, cultivation, and thinning; and to test different spacings and mixtures of trees.[6]

Along with silvicultural research, Pinchot continually concentrated on methods to promote forest protection. Fire was of course a major concern, and in the ensuing investigations, three relevant objectives were pursued: general reconnaissance of the extent and immediate damage done by forest fires considered to be national calamities, detailed studies on the ground of the effect of fires upon present and future forests and best methods for their prevention and control, and historical assessment of forest fires through compilation of available data.[7] Inquiries of this type were well exemplified in the spring of 1903 by the field trip on which Pinchot sent his foresters to the Adirondacks to survey the extent, causes, and effects of recent serious fires in the area. In extensive travels through the region, the foresters examined many of the burned areas and obtained information from guides, cruisers, lumbermen, pulp manufacturers, and superintendents of private forest lands. They also secured reports from fire wardens of all towns within or near the Adirondack Park and examined burned-over lands along the lines of the New York Central and the Delaware and Hudson Railroads.[8]

Insects injurious to forest growth have long claimed attention in protection and conservation programs. Work in this sector had been launched by A. D. Hopkins of the Bureau of Entomology, and, as early

---

[5] *Breaking New Ground*, p. 308.

[6] *Report of the Forester*, 1907, p. 23.

[7] Undated memorandum titled, "Forest Fires," prepared by the Office of Silvics, Bureau of Forestry, about 1904, Research Compilation File, RG 95.

[8] U.S.D.A., *Annual Reports, 1904*, p. 194.

as 1902, under Pinchot's guidance the Bureau of Forestry was cooperating on the problems. Primary focus was on life histories and depredations of forest insects in several important timber forest regions. A survey of damage by bark beetles to ponderosa pine stands in the Black Hills Forest Reserve, and development of control measures for these insects remain a landmark achievement in American forest entomological research.[9]

All these studies, conducted in the decade after 1898 by the Forest Service or its antecedents, had been instrumental in breaking new ground for American forest research and in inaugurating scientific practices on national forest lands. But the impermanence of the studies and the failure to recognize interrelated forest factors had constituted a major flaw in forestry policies and practices. These early shortcomings were illuminated when Raphael Zon formally brought them to Pinchot's attention in a paper titled "Plan for Creating Forest Experiment Stations" and dated May 6, 1908. Noting advantages of the systematic German organization of forest research work derived from established forest experiment stations beginning in 1870, Zon's paper called for their counterparts in American national forests where "experiments and studies leading to a full and exact knowledge of American silviculture, to the most economic utilization of the products of the forest, and to a fuller appreciation of the indirect benefits of the forest" could be pursued. Mindful of the deficiencies in past investigative work of the Forest Service, the paper recommended that each station be given "an area sufficient for the proper handling of short-period experiments, for experiments requiring a number of years, and for the maintenance of model forests typical of the silvicultural region." It was predicted that the experimental areas would furnish "valuable, instructive and convincing object lessons" to professional foresters, owners of forest lands, and especially national forest officers, and would provide demonstrations to laymen equally as appealing as those afforded already in scientific agricultural work.[10]

Pinchot gave Zon's plan almost immediate approval, probably because of his own favorable impression of European forest experiment stations and his high opinion of Zon's professional views — made manifest when in 1904 he appointed Zon chief of the newly renamed Office of Silvics. Pinchot's interest in European stations had been evidenced

[9] U.S.D.A., *Yearbook, 1949, Trees*, p. 428.

[10] Raphael Zon, "Plan for Creating Forest Experiment Stations," May 6, 1908 (unpublished), Research Compilation File, RG 95.

in 1906 when he accepted for the Forest Service membership in the International Association of Forest Experiment Stations. On that occasion he stated: "The Forest Service has always been deeply interested in the admirable work of the European experiment stations; which have been raising forestry from pure empirics to the position of a true science."[11]

Hence, July 1908 saw the establishment of the first federal forest experiment station in the Coconino National Forest near Flagstaff, Arizona, and a second station was created in 1909 near Manitou, Colorado. From these beginnings has evolved a program of regional forest and range experiment stations, each charged with the conduct of broad research for solution of forest and related range problems in a particular forest region. Though small and meagerly supported for a decade, these stations soon played a significant part in the Forest Service's solutions to difficult problems in artificial and natural reforestation in the arid West. In recent years they have taken a leading role in research for better production and management of forest resources in the principal timberland areas of the United States.

While Pinchot was inaugurating or expanding silvicultural studies to increase the productive power of forests, he was also promoting studies of forest products to determine their demand, supply, natural characteristics, and most profitable utilization. Such investigations had earlier been pursued by Fernow, but had been discontinued in 1896 at the direction of Secretary of Agriculture J. Sterling Morton, who doubted their practical value and relationship to the government's authorized work in forestry. Pinchot revived and broadened these studies, and his success was undoubtedly linked to his ability to demonstrate and publicize the economic value of federal forest work. In any event, as early as 1901 he arranged for dendrochemical analyses concerning tan extracts from native woods and a study of pulp woods to be done by the Bureau of Forestry in cooperation with the U.S. Agriculture Department's Bureau of Chemistry. In the same year, his Bureau and the Department's Bureau of Plant Industry undertook cooperative research. Authorized by Pinchot, this latter investigation dealt with conditions, causes, and prevention of decay in timbers, and for a few years was directed by Hermann von Schrenk, a plant pathologist at the Shaw School of Botany in St. Louis. Succeeding years of Pinchot's administration furthered research on the physical and me-

[11] Press Bulletin No. 144 of the Forest Service, December 17, 1906, RG 95.

chanical properties of commercially important woods, preservative treatment of these woods, problems in wood distillation, and utilization of new woods and mill waste in pulp manufacture. In these undertakings the Chief Forester relied heavily on cooperative work with engineers and other scientists at several universities, especially Yale, Purdue, and the Universities of California, Oregon, and Washington. Although lack of uniform procedures among the several research centers sometimes resulted in inconclusive findings, the work nonetheless has to its credit some of the earliest useful data for increasing the life of railway, telephone, mine, and other commercial timbers; providing standard specifications for such timbers; and understanding the protective action of creosote and other chemicals against wood-destroying fungi and marine borers.[12]

By 1909 the question of economic utilization of forest products had been brought into greater prominence by the national conservation movement with consequent demand for more effective research. The magnitude of the problems to be solved and deficiencies in existing heterogeneous and scattered research activities suggested strongly the desirability of concentrating forest products research in one institution. This view was confirmed in 1906 by McGarvey Cline, Pinchot's principal products specialist, in a methods survey in all of the cooperating products laboratories. Cline concluded that a central laboratory was needed to secure uniform standards in products research.

Pinchot agreed with Cline's findings and arranged a conference in Washington with representatives of the principal wood-using industries to discuss the need for a national wood-testing laboratory. Convening in November 1906, the conference members took steps to petition Congress for funds to establish such a laboratory under the control of the Forest Service. Subsequently, several bills seeking the necessary funds were introduced in Congress during 1907. When it appeared unlikely that Congress would take favorable action, Cline recommended the establishment of a central testing laboratory in cooperation with a prominent university. The Forest Service then invited several universities to make offers for a cooperative laboratory. In the bidding, rivalry between the University of Wisconsin and the University of Michigan was especially keen and Pinchot was subjected

---

[12] House of Representatives, 81st Congress, 2d Sess., Committee on Agriculture, *Research and Related Services in the U.S. Department of Agriculture* [Committee Print], II, 1643, 1649, 1694; U.S. Department of Agriculture, *Annual Reports, 1909*, pp. 412–413.

to considerable political pressure by Congressmen from these two states. After some indecision he accepted the offer from the University of Wisconsin, giving as his reasons the University's convenient location, good relations between the University and state and federal governments in conservation policies, and the institution's outstanding reputation for practical research under the leadership of President Charles R. Van Hise.[13] Thus on July 3, 1909, Pinchot signed an agreement with the President of the University's Board of Regents, W. D. Hoard, under which the University was to furnish a suitable building with heat, light, and power, while the Forest Service was to provide personnel, machinery, and raw materials.[14] In October Cline and other products research personnel moved to Madison and in June 1910 helped to open formally a laboratory that Pinchot accurately predicted would be "an important experimental center for all wood-using industries" and one of the "best equipped wood-testing laboratories of the world."[15]

Through the years, the Forest Products Laboratory at Madison has dealt with all phases of research concerning the structure, properties, treatment, and uses of wood. It has furnished highly useful information to wood-using industries at home and abroad and to the United States Government, especially during two world wars. Among its accomplishments proudly acclaimed by Pinchot were the opening of new sources of raw material and new technical processes to the pulp and paper industry, leadership in stimulating the use of wood preservatives, and pioneering work in the design and development of lumber dry kilns and glued plywood.[16] In a review of forestry research sponsored by the National Academy of Sciences during the 1920's two eminent scientists reported that the Laboratory already had become "generally recognized as the leading institution of its kind in the world" and was being used by several countries as a model for the organization of laboratories for forest utilization research.[17]

---

[13] For an excellent account of the background history of the Forest Products Laboratory, see Charles A. Nelson, "The Forest Products Laboratory," *Forest History*, xi (July 1967), pp. 6–14.

[14] Cooperative Agreement Between the University of Wisconsin and the Forester, July 3, 1909, Solicitor's Records, RG 16.

[15] U.S.D.A., *Annual Reports, 1909*, p. 412.

[16] *Breaking New Ground*, p. 313.

[17] I. W. Bailey and H. A. Spoehr, *The Role of Research in the Development of Forestry in America* (New York, 1929), p. 40.

XIII

Efforts for
Eastern National Forests

Pinchot's contribution to the creation of national forests in the eastern United States was one of the longer, unspectacular, yet significant, phases of the forest conservation movement that is often overlooked. This phase, beginning in the 1890's, more or less coincided with the first years of Pinchot's career as America's first professional forester, and he was soon actively supporting the project.

Perhaps the first person to suggest purchase by the federal government of lands in the East for the creation of national forests was Joseph A. Holmes, State Geologist of North Carolina and later Director of the United States Bureau of Mines. As early as 1892 or 1893 he was considering the matter with Pinchot.[1] Active efforts toward federal reservation and protection of certain eastern forest lands had originated with the Appalachian National Park Association, organized at Asheville, North Carolina, on November 22, 1899. This group promptly began to publicize the great advantages of the Southern Appalachians, its particular aim being to secure the establishment of a national park in western North Carolina and eastern Tennessee. To this association is to be credited the first organized movement to make some national use of the Southern Appalachians. It prepared and presented to Con-

---

[1] *Breaking New Ground,* p. 239.

gress a memorial calling attention to the region's rare natural beauty, excellent climate, and abundant forest and water resources and petitioned Congress to take steps to establish the proposed park. In this effort it enlisted the support of the Appalachian Mountain Club of Boston, Massachusetts, which also presented a similar memorial.

Upon the introduction of these memorials, Senator Pritchard of North Carolina in April 1900 secured an appropriation of $5,000 for a survey of forest conditions in the Southern Appalachian Mountains region of western North Carolina and adjacent states.[2] Means were thereby provided for a study of the Southern Appalachians by the Department of Agriculture and the United States Geological Survey. During the summer of 1900 officials of the Bureau of Forestry in cooperation with those of the Geological Survey investigated the Southern Appalachian Mountains from Virginia to Alabama, examining and mapping an area of 9,600,000 acres. In January 1901 the North Carolina state legislature passed a bill ceding to the federal government the right to acquire title to such lands as might be desired for forest reserve purposes and exempting the same from taxation. By the close of the year similar measures had been passed by legislative bodies in South Carolina, Tennessee, Virginia, and Georgia.

Meanwhile, in July 1901, Secretary of Agriculture Wilson accompanied by Pinchot, W J McGee, F. H. Newell, and J. A. Holmes spent ten days in the Southern Appalachian Mountains personally investigating sites proposed for an Appalachian national forest reserve. The deep, favorable impression which they gained from this trip made them warm advocates of federal aid in protecting and utilizing the forest resources of the Southern Appalachian region. The results of this investigation and the earlier field work by the Forestry Bureau and Geological Survey examiners were set forth in an elaborate report transmitted to Congress with a special message by President Roosevelt on December 19, 1901. This report, which formed the cornerstone of much of the later planning for national forests in this region, gave exhaustive data on the composition, condition, character, extent, and distribution of the forests of the Southern Appalachians, and advocated the purchase in this region of land for a national forest covering not less than four million acres.[3] Based largely upon this report or stimu-

---

[2] 31 Stat. L., 197.

[3] 57th Congress, 1st Sess., Senate Doc. No. 84, *Report of the Secretary of Agriculture in Relation to the Forests, Rivers and Mountains of the Southern Appalachian Region* (Washington, 1902).

lated by it, many articles appeared in magazines and newspapers, at once generating active interest in having Congress take affirmative action on the recommendation of the Secretary of Agriculture. Bills were introduced each session of Congress in both the Senate and House of Representatives and scarcely a year passed without large public hearings before committees on these bills. Some additional sentiment for these bills was stimulated undoubtedly by the American Forest Congress of 1905 which passed a resolution favoring the establishment of national forest reserves in the East. Addressing the Forest Congress Pinchot predicted: "We must have forest reserves, and we shall be forced to extend the area of forest reserves later on, not merely by Presidential proclamation, but by purchase."[4]

Meanwhile New England with its White Mountains began to claim equal consideration with the Southern Appalachians and joined forces in advocating establishment of national forests or parks in the eastern United States. Stimulated to activity by the wide public interest in this movement numerous government investigations were made. Three times the Senate passed a bill looking to the creation of a park or national forest, but no action could be secured in the House. In 1907, however, Congress did allocate $25,000 for a survey of the Southern Appalachian and White Mountain watersheds and a report on the advisability of their protection by national forests. The outcome was a map showing the nonagricultural regions of the southern mountains and an additional report to Congress by the Secretary of Agriculture. The report presented an enlarged concept of a series of national forests so located in the Southern Appalachians as to protect the headwaters of the principal streams from the Potomac and Monongahela to the Savannah.[5] Other scientific reports published by the federal government about the same time strengthened the popular demand, and the movement attained nationwide proportions. Practically all national and state organizations which gave attention to forestry questions passed resolutions favoring these national forests and sent representatives to advocate them at the Congressional hearings.

Pinchot was anxious to see these forests established as extensions of the national forest system already existing on public lands in the West. Through personal visits and reports of his assistants he had

[4] Press Bulletin No. 63 of the Forest Service, January 14, 1905, RG 95.
[5] 60th Congress, 1st Sess., Senate Doc., No. 91, *Report of the Secretary of Agriculture on the Southern Appalachian and White Mountain Watersheds* (Washington, 1908).

acquired considerable knowledge of the White Mountain forests. He knew much more about the forests of the Appalachian region; for since the days of his work at Biltmore he had studied large areas of them on foot and horseback and had carried a pack through many of them. Here where the southern and northern floras met, he pointed out, was the nation's richest and most varied body of hardwoods — timber sorely needed to supplement the dwindling national hardwood supply. Here also, much of the logging had destroyed the forests to a degree surpassed by that in few other forest areas of the United States. The need was urgent to provide conservative forest management for these eastern timberlands and, by reforestation of cut-over land, to assure future resources. With characteristic emphasis on economics, he told Congress that the purchase of the recommended forest areas would definitely "pay from a business point of view" just as existing national forests were doing.[6]

Because of a constitutional obstacle, however, Pinchot and others had to emphasize other reasons in their campaign for eastern forests. Under the federal Constitution, outstanding legal opinion suggested early that the creation of national forests by purchase was impossible. Arguments maintaining that this action could be taken under the general welfare clause of the Constitution were declared untenable. Foremost opinion was that the federal government could not engage in purchasing land for the direct purpose of creating national forests without an amendment of the Constitution. It was conceded, however, that this aim might possibly be attained by means of the Constitutional provision empowering Congress to regulate commerce among the several states. Under this provision protection of the navigable waterways was possible. Thus, if it could be proved that the creation of eastern forests would make the rivers originating in the watersheds covered by those forests more navigable, their acquisition seemed possible under the Constitution. As time went on Pinchot and other conservationists adopted this theory and gathered data designed to show the influence of forestation on the flow of rivers. By 1908 their supporters in Congress were regularly introducing bills for the creation of eastern national forests which were stated to have as their direct purpose the acquisition of forest and other lands for the protection of watersheds and the conservation of the navigability of navigable streams.

---

[6] Statement of Pinchot at a hearing on the Agricultural Appropriation Bill, Committee on Agriculture, House of Representatives, January 30, 1908.

In supporting these bills Pinchot argued that all the waters gathered in the Southern Appalachians flowed to the sea through navigable channels. He pointed out that the heavy rainfall and the steep slopes led to a very rapid run-off. There were no natural lakes for storage. If the flow were uniform, the amount of water discharged by these streams was sufficient to make their importance for navigation very high. But the run-off was variable and the variability was increasing. Furthermore, he maintained, all of the Southern Appalachian streams for which there were sufficient authentic records showed that floods were more frequent and of greater duration since the watersheds had been drastically stripped of their forestation by cutting and fire. Excessive periods of low waters also were increasing in length and frequency. The forest was the only natural influence tending to equalize the flow. Even on steep slopes the trees served to retard the flow, thus allowing time for moisture to filter below the surface and become underground drainage. In deforested areas the water instead of being absorbed was thrown off into streams in floods. With the rush of water down the slopes the soil was rapidly and steadily carried away, thereby causing fields to become gullied and streams silted and rendered less navigable.[7]

This argument concerning the influence of forests on the navigability of streams was vigorously opposed by a distinguished engineer of the United States Army, Hiram M. Chittenden. He denied the existence of any vital relationship between forest and river, as was claimed by Pinchot and other proponents of legislation for the creation of national forests in the East. Chittenden held that forests did not, and could not, exercise any controlling influence upon stream flow in times of great floods or extreme low water; that there had been higher high waters and lower waters in times before forests had been devastated; and that it was at least questionable that deforestation appreciably affected the silting of river channels. Citing the Mississippi River as an example, Chittenden maintained that its floods were due to precipitation rather than a lack of forestation. He conceded that the floods carried much eroded soil, but held that the greater part of it was brought down by the Missouri River which ran largely through flat, treeless, and often arid regions and carved out its large quantities of silt from its banks rather than from denuded and eroding watersheds.[8] Chitten-

[7] Press release of the Forest Service on the address of Pinchot before the Southern Commercial Congress, Washington, D.C., December 7, 1908.

[8] *Congressional Record*, February 9, 1909, pp. 2102–2121.

den's contentions were upheld substantially by Willis L. Moore, Chief
of the United States Weather Bureau, who also denied the existence of
any great influence of forestation on precipitation, in contradiction to
many forestry advocates.[9]

Another formidable obstacle to legislation for the eastern national
forests was evident in the person of Speaker Joseph G. Cannon of the
House of Representatives. To a friend, Pinchot confided his belief that
the Speaker was opposed to the legislation mainly because it was a
new thing. "I have found him consistently in opposition to novelty,
whether good or bad," the Forester complained and then added: "Mr.
Cannon finds it impossible . . . to assimilate any part of the new spirit
which has arisen in public affairs in the last few years."[10]

The sentiment for extending the national forest system to the eastern
States aroused by Pinchot and others was too great to be restrained by
the Chittenden-Moore point of view, strict Constitutional interpretation, or even Speaker Cannon. Consequently, Congress responded to
persistent public pressure and by the Weeks Act, approved March 1,
1911, provided for the establishment of national forests by land purchase on the watersheds of important navigable streams.[11] The law
was not limited to the Southern Appalachians and the White Mountains. Application of the law was restricted to lands which were to be
approved by the Geological Survey as being requisite for the protection of navigable streams, and to those States whose legislatures
granted authority to the federal government to acquire lands for this
purpose. It also provided for cooperative fire protection work of the
Forest Service with states and private forest owners. The Weeks Act
has been considered an epochal advance in American forest conservation efforts. It laid a foundation for two substantial national policies
which have since steadily and greatly expanded; namely, the policy of
extending national forests by purchase and that of fixing the pattern by
which the federal government cooperates with states and private owners in fire protection on private lands. Although the measure postdated
by a year his service as Forester, Pinchot was regarded as a "powerful
factor" in shaping this legislation and in securing its enactment.[12]

---

[9] Willis L. Moore, *Influence of Forests on Climate and on Floods* (Report of
the Committee on Agriculture, House of Representatives, 1910).

[10] Pinchot to Rev. D. D. Thompson, Editor, *Northwestern Christian Advocate*,
August 24, 1908, GPP.

[11] 36 Stat. L., 961.

[12] William L. Hall, "Hail to the Chief," *Journal of Forestry*, XLIII (August
1945), 556.

XIV

Apostle of Conservation

T HE SO-CALLED "conservation movement," to which Pinchot was so wholly dedicated, was in reality an outgrowth of earlier developments — forestry and reclamation policies, the work of the Public Lands Commission, coal land withdrawals, and agitation for improvement of waterways. The name of "conservation" does not appear to have been affixed to any part of this movement until the appointment of the Inland Waterways Commission in 1907. According to President Roosevelt, in each part of the movement Pinchot had been his "Chief Adviser" and the first person to suggest to him "courses which have actually proved so beneficial."[1] Progress toward conservation of all natural resources was undoubtedly advanced more by the forestry issue than by any other cause. As Van Hise and Havemeyer have pointed out: "The forests are the one natural resource whose rapid destruction made scientists realize as early as in the seventies that, if existing practice were continued, the end was in the not far distant future."[2]

Pinchot's untiring work in forestry widened the horizon to show why and how other natural resources should be protected and developed. In 1901 he collaborated with F. H. Newell, a Geological Survey engi-

[1] 60th Congress, 2d Sess., House of Representatives, Doc. No. 1425, *Proceedings of a Conference of Governors* (Washington, 1908), p. vi. Cited hereafter as *Proceedings of a Conference of Governors.*

[2] Charles R. Van Hise and Loomis Havemeyer, *Conservation of Our Natural Resources* (New York, 1936), p. 5.

neer, in drafting a part of President Roosevelt's first message to Congress which set forth the following views on forestry and irrigation:

> The forest and water problems are perhaps the most vital internal problems of the United States. . . . The forests alone cannot, however, fully regulate and conserve the waters of the arid region. Great storage works are necessary to equalize the flow of streams and to save the flood waters. Their construction has been conclusively shown to be an undertaking too vast for private effort. Nor can it be best accomplished by the individual States acting alone. These irrigation works should be built by the National Government. The lands reclaimed by them should be reserved by the Government for actual settlers, and the cost of construction should so far as possible be repaid by the land reclaimed.[3]

In this recommendation can be seen the basic policy that was enacted in 1902 by Nevada Senator Francis G. Newlands' reclamation bill. Pinchot's part in this legislative achievement apparently consisted mainly of helping Newell and Newlands to furnish pro-reclamation facts and arguments for Congressmen. As usual, his role seemingly was to generate support and enthusiasm. Thomas F. Walsh, president of the Trans-Mississippi Commercial Congress, commented: "He even pushed aside for the time being his cherished forest preservation ambition so he could devote his whole time, energy and influence to preaching the gospel of reclamation. In the winter of 1901 there was no more loyal, faithful, and harder worker in . . . Washington in this good cause, outside of President Roosevelt than Gifford Pinchot."[4]

This effort for reclamation, his prior experience as a member of the National Forest Commission, and forest surveys for the Department of the Interior had given Pinchot a fund of knowledge of public-land laws. From this broad perspective he was able to deduce not only that most of these laws were defective, but that they were badly administered by the General Land Office. Being especially anxious to show how that administration was detrimental to the public forest lands, he suggested to President Roosevelt that a commission be named to study the situation.[5] The President agreed, and on October 22, 1903,

---

[3] *Messages and Papers of the Presidents*, xiv, 6658.
[4] Speech of Walsh to the Denver Chamber of Commerce, October 29, 1908, as reported in the Denver *Republican*, October 30, 1908.
[5] *Breaking New Ground*, pp. 243–244.

appointed a Public Lands Commission "to report upon the condition, operation, and effect of the present land laws, and to recommend such changes as are needed to effect the largest practicable disposition of the public lands to actual settlers who will build permanent homes upon them, and to secure in permanence the fullest and most effective use of the resources of the public lands." [6] Members of the Commission were W. A. Richards, commissioner of the General Land Office, who was named chairman, F. H. Newell, and Pinchot, who was secretary. Pinchot thanked the President for the "great and welcome duty" given him by the appointment. [7]

This was indeed no small assignment, for in 1903 the public lands still embraced vast regions covering *in toto* nearly one-third of the entire area of the United States. Widely scattered, extending from the Gulf of Mexico to the Pacific and from Canada to Mexico, these lands included every variety of topography and climate. Excluding Alaska, there were twenty-three states and three territories which contained public lands in amounts varying from 5 to 95 per cent of their land surfaces. [8] After hearing testimony for several weeks in Washington, early in 1904 Newell and Pinchot began field investigations by attending meetings of the National Livestock Association and the National Wool Growers Association in Portland, Oregon. They also visited Sacramento, California; Reno, Nevada; Salt Lake City, Utah; Denver, Colorado; and Cheyenne, Wyoming, where they conferred with governors, state land boards, other public officials, and various citizens on different aspects of public-land laws.

The Public Lands Commission made two partial reports. In the first one, presented on March 7, 1904, Pinchot's ideas were unmistakable. It recommended changes in the public-land laws that related mainly to the control, use, and disposal of forest lands. It urged, for example, the repeal of the Timber and Stone Act, under which public timberland could be purchased for $2.50 an acre and almost immediately transferred to a lumber company or land speculator. In place of this law the Commission recommended that Congress authorize the Secretary of the Interior to sell timber on any unappropriated, nonmineral, surveyed lands at public auction to the highest bidder, who would be forbidden to sell it again without the Secretary's permission. It also

[6] 58th Congress, 3d Sess., Senate Doc. No. 189 (Washington, 1905), p. iii.
[7] Pinchot to Roosevelt, October 27, 1903, General Correspondence, RG 95.
[8] 58th Congress, 3d Sess., Senate Doc. No. 189, p. iv.

suggested that in forest reserves lands that were found to be chiefly valuable for agriculture might be opened for homestead entry, but that such lands should not be subject to commutation (that is, purchase after fourteen month's residence, or exchange under the much criticized Lieu-Land Law).

The second partial report was transmitted to Congress by the President on February 13, 1905, with his general approval. This report recommended the purchase of private lands inside forest reserves rather than exchange under the Lieu-Land Law; reiterated its recommendation for the repeal of the Timber and Stone Act; suggested the sale of timber from unreserved public lands; advised three years' residence under the commutation clause of the Homestead Act and, under the Desert Land Act, two years' residence with actual production of a valuable crop.

In addition, grazing practices advocated by the Public Lands Commission were particularly well-documented. Not only were the members familiar with the problem, but their recommendations were based on a study of grazing systems of Texas and Wyoming, the Union Pacific Railroads, and the Indian Office; on a conference with representative stockmen from the various grazing-land states and territories; on 1,400 answers to a circular letter to stockmen throughout the West; and on facts and opinions gathered at various meetings, interviews, and from correspondence. The Commission recommended that authority be given to the President to set aside by proclamation certain grazing districts or reserves, and to the Secretary of Agriculture to regulate and charge a moderate fee for grazing, with the special aim of effecting the greatest permanent occupation of the country by actual home makers.

The recommendations of this second report were the final ones made by the Commission. Pinchot was doubtless much too busy for further work with that group because, five days before the transmittal of the report to Congress, administration of the federal forests had at last been transferred to his Bureau. As he saw it, there was little need for more reporting, since his great objective had now been achieved.

The Commission's recommendations brought no immediate changes in the existing public-land laws. The chief value of its work lay in the information and experience gained by Pinchot and the other members who were brought into direct contact with problems involving the use of all the natural resources of the public domain. It may well be, as Pinchot suggested, that the Public Lands Commission "had a part in planting and watering the seed which developed into the world-wide policy of Conservation."[9]

Valuable coal lands on the public domain had for several years been passing into private hands under the agricultural land laws. President Roosevelt believed that unless this situation was changed, all the coal of the country would soon be in the hands of a few monopolistic companies with some such general trust control as was then exercised over oil by the Standard Oil Company.[10] Thus in an order of June 29, 1906, he directed Secretary of the Interior Hitchcock to withdraw from entry for examination and classification all public land considered "as probably containing workable deposits of coal." Pursuant to this order between July 28, 1906, and November 12, 1906, there were withdrawn from entry 66,000,000 acres of public land.[11]

This withdrawal of coal lands was accomplished with the full approval and active support of the Forest Service. On April 2, 1906, William Loeb, Jr., Secretary to the President, had addressed an inquiry to Pinchot seeking his views as to whether the President might reserve specifically described tracts of coal land from entry or disposition under the general land laws and whether he might withdraw all vacant coal lands in the United States or in any described locality from disposition under such laws.[12] To this inquiry Pinchot replied, on the basis of an opinion prepared by Woodruff, his legal adviser, that the President unquestionably could lawfully reserve specifically described tracts of coal land as exigencies of the public service required. The cases of Grisar v. McDowell (6 Wall. p. 380), Wolsey v. Chapman (101 U.S., 755, p. 768), and Wilcox v. Jackson (13 Peters 498) were cited as proof of this authority. The Chief Forester also felt that an order withdrawing from entry or disposition all vacant coal lands of the United States could also be upheld legally. Moreover, he stated that the acquisition of large tracts of coal lands in northwestern Colorado and in Utah by and on behalf of railroad companies and other corporations was "a matter of public comment" in those States.[13]

In September 1906, Associate Forester Price informed Pinchot that only a few townships of forest reserve land had been included in the coal land withdrawals authorized by the President. The result, he re-

[9] *Breaking New Ground*, p. 250.
[10] Pinchot to August Wolf, March 2, 1907, Law Office Correspondence, RG 95.
[11] U.S. Department of the Interior, *Annual Reports*, 1907, I, 251.
[12] Loeb to Pinchot, April 14, 1906, General Correspondence, RG 95.
[13] Pinchot to Loeb, April 14, 1906, General Correspondence, RG 95.

ported, had been "to stampede would-be-owners of coal land into frantic efforts to locate the areas not yet withdrawn." Thus he urged Pinchot to request the President to make immediate withdrawal of the coal lands in the national forests.[14] The Chief Forester, who was then making an inspection trip in Idaho, immediately sent a telegram to the President advising him strongly to withdraw coal lands in the public forests.[15] When he returned to Washington in October he further urged the President to make withdrawals of coal lands. On this advice and the approval of the Geological Survey, Roosevelt ordered the withdrawal of about 40,000,000 acres, 10,000,000 of which were located in the national forests.[16]

A further step in the gathering force of the conservation movement was the appointment of the Inland Waterways Commission in 1907. Although President Roosevelt had credited Pinchot with the idea for such a commission,[17] Pinchot indicated in his autobiography that the idea probably originated with W J McGee,[18] a distinguished geologist and ethnologist, whose geological investigations under the celebrated Major John W. Powell had attracted considerable attention.[19] In any event the plan for the Commission became a joint undertaking in which Pinchot and McGee worked out the details and selected the members to be recommended for appointment. After they had submitted the plan to the President and obtained his approval, their strategy was to induce a public demand that would justify the President's setting up this Commission. This was not difficult, since businessmen interested in water transportation and other uses of waterways had already organized numerous promotional associations. Outstanding among these, the Lakes-to-the-Gulf Deep Waterway Association, headquartered in St. Louis, sent vigorous and effective petitions to Washington urging an investigation of the nation's waterways systems.

In a letter of March 14, 1907, creating the Inland Waterways Commission, President Roosevelt stated that his action was "influenced by broad considerations of national policy." He pointed out that the con-

---

[14] O. W. Price to Pinchot, September 15, 1906, General Correspondence, RG 95.

[15] Pinchot to Price, September 20, 1906, General Correspondence, RG 95.

[16] G. W. Woodruff to Price, October 24, 1906, Law Office Correspondence, RG 95.

[17] Speech of President Roosevelt at Jamestown, Va., June 10, 1907, Proceedings of a Conference of Governors, p. vi.

[18] McGee wrote his name without periods after the W and J since these letters were actually a given name rather than initials.

[19] Breaking New Ground, p. 327.

trol of navigable waterways lies with the federal government and carries with it corresponding responsibilities. It was becoming clear that streams should be considered and conserved as great natural resources. Works designed to control American waterways had been undertaken usually for a single purpose, such as the improvement of navigation, development of power, irrigation of arid lands, protection of lowlands from floods, or to supply water for domestic and manufacturing purposes. The time had come, the President felt, to merge "local projects and uses of the nation's inland waters in a comprehensive plan designed for the benefit of the entire country." Since such a plan should take into account the orderly development of other natural resources, the Commission was asked to "consider the relation of streams to the use of all the great permanent natural resources and their conservation for the making and maintenance of prosperous homes." [20]

Roosevelt named the chairman of the Rivers and Harbors Committee of the House of Representatives, Theodore E. Burton of Ohio, to be chairman of the Inland Waterways Commission. The vice-chairman, elected by the Commission, was Senator Francis G. Newlands, author of the bill which created the Reclamation Service and chairman of the Senate Committee on Interstate Commerce. The other members were Senator William Warnor of Missouri; Senator John H. Bankhead of Alabama; General Alexander Mackenzie, Chief of the Corps of Engineers of the United States Army; Herbert Knox Smith, head of the Federal Bureau of Corporation; F. H. Newell, leader in the movement for reclamation and head of the Reclamation Service; McGee and Pinchot. Principal credit for the work performed by the Commission belongs to McGee, who served as its Secretary, and Smith who supervised the compilation of most of the 664 pages of appendix to its report.

The work of the Inland Waterways Commission began on April 29, 1907, in the United States Capitol. From May to October it made inspection trips on the Mississippi River, one from St. Louis to New Orleans and the Passes, another from St. Paul to Memphis, and one on the Missouri River from Kansas City to St. Louis. Desiring to impress upon the public the need for inland waterway improvement, the Commission invited President Roosevelt to make a trip down the Mississippi River with it and the Mississippi Valley Improvement Association which offered to provide steamboats for the trip. The President accepted the invitation and was met by the Commission at Keokuk, Iowa,

---

[20] 60th Congress, 1st Sess., Senate Doc. No. 325, *Preliminary Report of the Inland Waterways Commission* (Washington, 1908), pp. 15–16.

Governor Pinchot representing Pennsylvania in the Inaugural Parade, March 4, 1925, when Calvin Coolidge began his second term as President of the United States. (p. 146)

Gifford Pinchot, at work on his autobiography, *Breaking New Ground*, cele-brates his eightieth birthday anniversary, August 11, 1945. (p. 149)

on October 1, 1907. There also the governors of twelve States joined the party and ten more governors at St. Louis. The trip of this distinguished group down the Mississippi was a great publicity stroke. The party was given a tremendously friendly reception all along the river. A photograph of Pinchot telling a story to the President on the deck of one of the ships was circulated widely by the press and showed the close friendship existing between the two men. On October 4, the flotilla arrived at Memphis, where the President addressed a convention of the Lakes-to-the-Gulf Deep Waterway Association, and announced that he intended to call a national conference on the conservation of natural resources.

The Commission returned to Washington in November 1907 and issued a "preliminary" (but actually a final) report, prepared mainly by McGee, in February 1908. It noted that some 25,000 miles of navigated rivers and an equal amount which might be made navigable, some 2,500 miles of navigable canals, and over 25,000 miles of sounds, bays and bayous, readily connectable by canals, indicated the great possibilities of inland navigation in the United States. It pointed out the need to develop and coordinate this navigation with railways to meet the full national requirements of transportation. Improvement of inland waterways would increase the purity and supply of water for domestic and commercial uses, lead to the construction of engineering works essential for the prevention of floods and low waters, and help to prevent great losses from soil erosion. It was desirable "to continue the collection of data with a view to so adjusting irrigation and power development with navigation as to secure the highest value of the water to the greatest number of people." Finally, the Commission found that the unsurpassed natural wealth and the eagerness of the American people for immediate results regardless of future needs had "led to a policy of extravagant consumption of national resources and to an encouragement of monopoly" whereby an excessive share of such resources had been "diverted to the enrichment of the few rather than preserved for the equitable benefit of the many." These monopolistic tendencies could be seen in extensive control of mineral fuels on public lands, acquisition and needless destruction of forests, seizure of valuable waterpower sites, and control of production and transportation facilities.[21]

In its recommendations the Inland Waterways Commission urged

---

[21] 6oth Congress, 1st Sess., Senate Doc. No. 325, pp. 18–25.

the acceptance of a principle that has since become a fundamental concept in American planning for the use of water resources. It maintained in effect that every river is a unit from its source to its mouth. If it is to be handled successfully so that it can be used for all the purposes by which it can serve the people, it must be treated as a unit. Thus, plans for the improvement of navigation in inland waterways, or for any use of these waterways in connection with interstate commerce should take account of the purification of the waters, development of power, control of floods, reclamation of lands by irrigation and drainage, and all other uses or benefits to be obtained from their control. The Commission recommended that the President be authorized by Congress to create a National Waterways Commission to coordinate the work of various federal agencies affecting inland waterways and to continue the investigation of questions relating to the improvement and utilization of these waterways and related natural resources. To Pinchot the Commission's most important recommendation was "that hereafter any plans for the use of inland waterways . . . shall regard the streams of the country as an asset of the people, shall take full account of the conservation of all resources connected with running waters and shall look to the protection of these resources from monopoly and to their administration in the interests of the people."[22]

In transmitting the report of the Inland Waterways Commission to Congress on February 26, 1908, President Roosevelt called it a "thorough, conservative, sane, and just" statement on a subject of critical importance both to the present and the future of the United States. He urged further investigation of the problem of inland waterways with a view to the development of a definite and progressive policy and declared that the development of waterways and the conservation of forests were the "two most pressing physical needs of the country."[23] In the words of Pinchot, the report may properly be called "one of the great Conservation documents of American history," for it embodied basic concepts that eventually have had a great influence on public policy relating to natural resources. Upon some of these views would be based, a generation later, one of the greatest waterways developments of all times, the Tennessee Valley Authority.[24] More immediate, though, was the value of the Inland Waterways Commission in its suggestion for the conference that brought the early

---

[22] Senate Doc. No. 325, p. 25–27.
[23] Senate Doc. No. 325, pp. iii–vii.
[24] Ise, *United States Forest Policy*, p. 151.

conservation movement to a climax — the Conference of Governors, in May 1908.

The proposal for the conference can perhaps be credited to the efforts of a number of devoted conservationists. One of them was R. U. Johnson of the *Century Magazine*. As early as August 1906 he had urged President Roosevelt to convene the governors of the eastern states for consideration of a forest conservation policy.[25] At any rate, in May 1907 during its period of initial activity, the Inland Waterways Commission had discussed the desirability of a conservation conference and resolved to seek the President's approval of such a meeting. Not unexpectedly, Pinchot was named a member of a committee to approach the President, who readily endorsed the proposal.

The Conference of Governors was convened and in his opening address, May 13, 1908, President Roosevelt lauded Pinchot's initiative, energy, devotion, and farsightedness in the conservation movement and declared: "If it had not been for him this convention neither would nor could have been called."[26] In those days, this meeting was one of the most notable gatherings ever assembled in Washington, attended not only by most of the governors but also by other leaders in diverse fields of endeavor. The list of speakers read like a roster of "Who's Who" in American public life, for it included, in addition to the President, such notables as Elihu Root, William Jennings Bryan, Andrew Carnegie, James J. Hill, Samuel Gompers, Charles Evans Hughes, and Seth Low. The historic conference urged the immediate adoption of conservation practices to check the exhaustion of the nation's forest and mineral resources and to utilize more effectively its waterways. It led to the preparation of a comprehensive inventory of the country's natural resources by the National Conservation Commission, created by Roosevelt in June 1908 and headed by Pinchot.

In this inventory the National Conservation Commission reported that forests in the United States by 1908 covered about 550,000,000 acres, or about one fourth of the land area of the country. The original forests had covered not less than 850,000,000 acres. The publicly owned forests contained one-fifth of the nation's standing timber, while the privately owned forests had the remainder — and generally more valuable timber. But scientific forestry was being practiced on less than one per cent of the privately owned forests. Since 1870 forest fires had

---

[25] R. U. Johnson to Roosevelt, August 28, 1906, Law Office Correspondence, RG 95.

[26] *Proceedings of a Conference of Governors*, p. 3.

destroyed a yearly average of $50,000,000 worth of timber. The young growth destroyed by fire was worth far more than the marketable timber burned. Not counting the loss by fire, Americans took from the forests each year three and a half times as much timber as their yearly growth. This drain was in marked contrast with the practice in European countries such as France and Germany, where scientific forestry was more widely practiced. Unlike most advanced nations, America still taxed privately owned forests under a general property tax which tended to prevent reforestation and perpetuation of existing forests by use. It was suggested that it was far better that forest land should be subject to a moderate tax permanently than that it should provide an excessive revenue temporarily and then cease to pay at all. The Commission warned, as Pinchot had done for a decade, that the conservative use of the forest and of timber by Americans would not be widespread until they learned how to practice forestry.

The national movement for the conservation of natural resources soon acquired, in a sense, continental proportions. Here again, Pinchot played a leading role. It was he who suggested to President Roosevelt that a North American Conservation Conference should be held, and who carried the President's personal invitation to Lord Grey, Governor General of Canada, and President Porfirio Diaz of Mexico. Canada, the colony of Newfoundland, and Mexico immediately accepted, and the representatives convened at the White House on February 18, 1909, with Pinchot as Chairman. The conference adopted a statement declaring that no nation acting alone could adequately conserve national resources, which are not confined by national boundary lines, and hence recommended the adoption of concurrent measures to conserve these resources and determine their location and extent. It suggested that the President of the United States should invite all nations to join in a "conference on the subject of world resources and their inventory, conservation, and wise utilization." [27]

Even before the North American Conservation Conference had made its recommendation for a world meeting on conservation, Secretary of State Elihu Root in January 1909 had informally inquired of the principal foreign governments as to whether they would favor an invitation to send delegates to such a conference. Responses to the inquiry were said to be uniformly favorable. Accordingly, with the concurrence of the Netherlands, invitations were sent by President Roosevelt to fifty-eight nations to assemble at the Peace Palace in The

---

[27] 60th Congress, 2d Sess., Senate Doc. No. 742 (Washington, 1909).

Hague in September 1909. More than half of them had accepted invitations when Roosevelt left office in March 1909.[28] President Taft, however, withdrew the invitations and by the time the proposed world conference was to have been in session Pinchot was in controversy with a member of the new President's Cabinet that was to lead to his dismissal from service in the federal government. How successful such a world conference might have been at that time can be only a matter of speculation. Great Britain had accepted President Roosevelt's invitation, but American Ambassador to Britain Whitelaw Reid reported that some men in the Foreign Office had expressed "bewilderment as to what such a Congress (World Conference) was wanted for and what it could probably do."[29] Over the years Pinchot continued to urge his plan on successive Presidents, but he did not live to see the realization of this special goal. In 1949, three years after Pinchot's death, the United Nations, at President Truman's request, did hold a world conservation meeting at Lake Success, New York. Speaking to the delegates on August 19, United States Secretary of Agriculture Charles F. Brannan declared:

> It was a number of years ago that a session and an international congress of this kind was first conceived. It was if I understand correctly, probably first suggested by a great American conservationist, the Honorable Gifford Pinchot. . . . It was Gifford Pinchot who first brought to the American people's attention the importance of our forest resources and who began to direct and guide the thinking of some others, a very few people in the first instance, towards the relationship between the maintenance of a strong economy and society in this country or in any country and the effective use of its soil and other natural resources. So, I would like to take this occasion to pay my respects to a great conservationist, who has unfortunately left us behind with this task.[30]

---

[28] *Breaking New Ground*, pp. 366–367.

[29] Reid to Pinchot, August 23, 1909, Conservation Congress Correspondence, RG 95.

[30] United Nations, Department of Economic Affairs, *Proceedings of the United Nations Scientific Conference on the Conservation and Utilization of Resources* (New York, 1950), I, 72.

XV

Discord and Dismissal

URING Theodore Roosevelt's administration, that ended in March 1909, the conservation movement under Pinchot's leadership was being enthusiastically supported by the President as well as most governors of the states, industrial leaders, and numerous private organizations. But it was receiving little approval and often active opposition in Congress. The attitude of Congress was manifest in its treatment of appropriations for the National Conservation Commission. Complying with a request by the outgoing President for such funds, Senator Knute Nelson of Minnesota in February 1909 introduced an amendment to the Sundry Civil Bill appropriating $25,000 for expenses of the Commission.[1] The amendment was rejected by the Senate Committee on Appropriations. Not content with denying the Commission operating funds, Congress in the ensuing Taft administration placed in the Sundry Civil Bill a clause which prohibited all federal bureaus from doing work for any commission, board, or similar body appointed by the President without legislative sanction. Representative James A. Tawney of Minnesota, a persistent opponent of conservation, authored this measure against the continuance of the National Conservation Commission's work. He contended that Roosevelt had appointed various commissions without any sanction of Congress and that this was channeling the work of some of the federal agencies into courses other than those intended by Congress.[2] Not only

[1] *Congressional Record*, February 17, 1909, p. 2561.
[2] *Congressional Record*, July 27, 1909, p. 4614.

did Congress force the discontinuance of the National Conservation Commission, but it also refused to take any immediate action on the Commission's detailed survey of timber resources and related matters. Thus, despite his zealous efforts, Pinchot had to admit, in October 1909, ten months after the Commission had made its report: "No action has as yet been taken by Congress on the Report of the National Conservation Commission. Movements of this kind make progress only when they are backed by strong public opinion. . . . It takes time and propaganda work to bring the people as a whole to realize the full importance of such problems."[3]

In subsequent months, this setback paled to relative insignificance with the enacting of one of the most dramatic and consequential episodes in American political history — the Ballinger-Pinchot controversy. The details are well known and have been set forth at length in several studies of varying objectivity.[4] The dispute was concerned not mainly with forests, but rather with coal and waterpower. It seems necessary to mention it in this account because of its imagined and real effect on Pinchot's forestry program and career.

As a backdrop to the stormily emotion-charged sequelae, Richard A. Ballinger in 1907 — then Commissioner of the General Land Office and a member of the Public Lands Commission — had disagreed with the opinion of Chief Forester Pinchot and F. H. Newell that the coal lands of Alaska should be leased rather than sold.[5] These differences in inter-

---

[3] Pinchot to M. René Tavernier, October 14, 1909, Office of Silvics Correspondence, RG 95.

[4] Rose M. Stahl, *The Ballinger-Pinchot Controversy* (Northampton, 1926) is an early detailed account of the controversy. Fairly objective but less comprehensive is John T. Ganoe, "Some Constitutional and Political Aspects of the Ballinger-Pinchot Controversy," *Pacific Historical Review*, III (September 1934), 323–333. Provocative but on the whole less objective are A. T. Mason, *Bureaucracy Convicts Itself* (New York, 1941), a pro-Pinchot account, and Harold L. Ickes (U.S. Dept. of Interior Publications), *Not Guilty* (Washington, 1940), a pro-Ballinger treatment. Political, economic, and administrative aspects of the controversy are ably dealt with by Elmo R. Richardson, *The Politics of Conservation* (Berkeley and Los Angeles, 1962), M. Nelson McGeary, *Gifford Pinchot, Forester-Politician* (Princeton, 1960), and Samuel P. Hays, *Conservation and the Gospel of Efficiency* (Cambridge, 1959). A recent analysis of Ballinger's administrative and political philosophy is presented by James L. Penick, Jr., "The Age of the Bureaucrat, Another View of the Ballinger-Pinchot Controversy," *Forest History*, VII (Spring–Summer 1963), 15–21.

[5] 61st Congress, 3d Sess., Senate Doc. No. 719, *Investigation of the Interior Department and of the Bureau of Forestry* (Washington, 1911), IV, 1146, 1157. This work will be cited hereafter as *Interior and Forestry Investigation*.

pretation had served to arouse Pinchot's doubts of Ballinger's loyalty to the cause of conservation.

President Roosevelt's Secretary of the Interior had been James R. Garfield. One of Pinchot's staunchest supporters, he had been the enabling factor in many of the conservation measures that Pinchot sought but which, as a subordinate official in another department, he could not put into operation. The outgoing President and Pinchot had believed that President Taft would reappoint Garfield to his same cabinet post in the new administration.

Taft instead appointed a corporation lawyer, the same Richard Ballinger whose loyalties to conservation had already come into question. Not only was Ballinger expected to provide desirable representation of the West in the Taft cabinet,[6] but his interpretations of conservation policy were favored over Garfield's. Taft's appointment of four additional corporation lawyers to the cabinet did nothing to allay the growing apprehensions of conservationists. The sum of these events seemed to indicate that such cabinet members would be little inclined to combat monopolistic control of natural resources. In April 1909 the premonitions among western conservationists were described by F. H. Newell:

> The people in the West seem to be somewhat apprehensive of a reaction and are predicting a counter current of public sentiment if the men now in charge carry out their ideas of doing things "differently." The Washington correspondents have given out the conception that the new administration is too much impressed with the necessity of conciliating the great interests and that the little man will have very little show! I am embarrassed by leading questions as to why Garfield is out. . . . His successor will have a hard time getting any general appreciation.[7]

The Taft administration brought with it an opposing concept of the federal government's proper role in implementing a conservation program. Whereas the Roosevelt-Pinchot interpretation — broad, dynamic, and often impatient of the restraint of legal methods — had assumed that a public official could and should do anything in the public interest that the law did not specifically forbid him to do, President Taft and Secretary Ballinger now adhered to a strict legalistic view which obliged an administrative official to confine himself to doing only what

---

[6] Henry F. Pringle, *The Life and Times of William Howard Taft* (New York, 1939), II, 478.

[7] Newell to Pinchot, April 26, 1909, GPP.

the law specifically permitted or directed. From this standpoint, the new President believed some of Garfield's conservation policies had been of doubtful legality. This basic conflict in ideas was often obscured by the clash of personal and political loyalties that followed. Against this background, and less than a month after President Taft took office in March 1909, the controversy between Pinchot and Ballinger came out into the open in the issue of waterpower sites, when Ballinger began restoring withdrawn sites to entry.[8]

Earlier, Garfield had withdrawn extensive waterpower sites from entry, under the theory of "the general supervisory power of the Executive" over the public domain — a theory previously formulated largely by George Woodruff. After Congress had failed to provide necessary public land legislation as recommended by the Public Lands Commission and Roosevelt, it had become necessary, as Roosevelt saw it, "to use what law was already in existence, and further to supplement it by Executive action."[9] Garfield had readily accepted this theory and by 1908 had enunciated his own version of it, which he called the "stewardship" of the Executive over the public domain.[10]

Ballinger now took the position that Garfield's withdrawals were beyond the intent of existing legislation. Accordingly, on March 20, 1909, the new Secretary of the Interior began restoring the withdrawn sites to entry, in rejection of Garfield's basic stewardship principle. Ballinger's argument was later spelled out in his contention:

> By the Constitution, Congress is made the steward of the public domain and for its stewardship it is responsible to the people. In selling or otherwise disposing of this national estate the executive can move only as directed or authorized by Congress. . . . Consequently the movement to conserve the national resources in this national estate . . . is a matter with which Congress must deal.[11]

Pinchot immediately interpreted Ballinger's restorations as a reversal of Rooseveltian conservation policy. He conferred with President Taft three times between April 19 and April 22, 1909, and explained the significance of Ballinger's action.[12] Following these conferences, the President discussed the power-site question with Ballinger and ap-

[8] *Interior and Forestry Investigation*, I, 71, 76.
[9] Theodore Roosevelt, *Autobiography*, p. 441.
[10] U.S. Department of the Interior, *Annual Reports, 1908*, I, 12–13.
[11] U.S. Department of the Interior, *Annual Reports, 1910*, I, 11–12.
[12] *Interior and Forestry Investigation*, VI, 4207.

parently directed him to rewithdraw power sites. On April 23 the Secretary issued instructions for specific rewithdrawals based upon information furnished by the Geological Survey. The acreage thus rewithdrawn amounted to 421,129 acres, as contrasted with the 3,450,460 acres previously withdrawn by Garfield without accurate surveys — and consequently containing considerable privately owned land and some public land not bordering on streams. Despite the smaller acreage represented by the Ballinger rewithdrawals, more sites actually useful for waterpower purposes were covered than by the larger area withdrawn by his predecessor.[13]

Differences between the Chief Forester and the new Secretary of the Interior also arose over the question of ranger station withdrawals. Secretaries Hitchcock and Garfield had regularly granted requests from the Forest Service for the withdrawal of tracts of land, ranging from one hundred to two hundred acres, in or near national forests, to be used as headquarters for forest rangers. The requests were granted on the theory that such tracts were to be used as administrative sites and could be legally withdrawn in the same way as sites for federal arsenals or lighthouses. In reality, however, as Pinchot himself later acknowledged: "A certain number of Ranger stations were applied for which were needed less for Rangers than to give the Government a temporary hold on some power site."[14] Garfield affirmed that he had granted, with the complete approval of President Roosevelt, such applications "to prevent the illegal acquisition of sites by water power companies under the mineral laws."[15]

By the time Ballinger became Secretary of the Interior in 1909, approximately 20,000 acres had been withdrawn outside the national forests for ranger stations and about 580,000 acres for similar purposes within the national forests. Soon he was confronted with several hundred applications for more withdrawals for ranger stations. After April 15, 1909, he rejected all of these applications. He contended that such withdrawals in national forests conflicted with mining rights under an act of Congress and that withdrawals outside national forests in Oregon, Washington, Idaho, Montana, Colorado, and Wyoming would constitute additions to national forests which were prohibited without Congressional approval.[16] He held steadfastly to this view

---

[13] *Interior and Forestry Investigation*, I, 71.
[14] *Breaking New Ground*, p. 411.
[15] Garfield to Pinchot, May 8, 1909, Ballinger-Pinchot Controversy records, RG 95.
[16] *Interior and Forestry Investigation*, V, 1528.

despite Pinchot's argument that the ranger stations were administrative sites.

Still another conflict ensued over a cooperative agreement of January 23, 1908, which had provided that the Forest Service should undertake the protection of the forests on the Indian reservations and supervise the sale and cutting of timber. The salaries and expenses of the men actually employed were paid for by the Indian Office of the Interior Department, but the men were considered Forest Service employees and therefore subject to its supervision. This arrangement apparently had the full approval of President Roosevelt and conformed with his desire for full cooperation between federal departments. While it lasted, considerable progress was made in establishing forest protection methods on the Indian reservations.[17] Ballinger, however, being dissatisfied with this arrangement because the employees remained under Pinchot's supervision, abrogated the cooperative agreement on the ground that a ruling of the Comptroller made it illegal to detail employees from one department to another. This ruling of September 3, 1908, had related to the detailing of a clerk under the cooperative agreement from the Forest Service to the Indian Office. To no avail, Pinchot maintained that it did not apply to the long-established custom of the Comptroller to allow departments to do special work for each other provided they did the work at cost.[18]

The feud between Pinchot and Ballinger reached its greatest intensity over the already mentioned issue of the administration of the Alaskan coal fields. Opened to entry by an act of Congress in 1900, amended in 1904, these lands were restricted to a claim of 160 acres per person which involved the "staking out" or location of the claim, filing a notice of such location, improvement of the claim, and the presentation of an affidavit of good faith by each claimant. When these provisions had been complied with, claimants could receive certificates of entry. If the claims were found to be proper, they were "clear-listed." In 1906 the Alaskan coal lands were withdrawn along with similar areas in the continental United States. Of the 900 claims located by then, only 33 had received certificates of entry by 1909. These 33 claims became known as the Cunningham claims, taking their name from Clarence Cunningham, the agent responsible for locating them. Before they were "clear-listed" their validity was investigated by H. K. Love, a Special Agent of the General Land Office, from December 11, 1905,

[17] *Breaking New Ground*, p. 412.
[18] Stahl, *The Ballinger-Pinchot Controversy*, pp. 86–88.

to June 21, 1907. In the process of this investigation, Love received complaints of fraudulent practices by the Alaska coal claimants, which pointed to an arrangement made by the Cunningham group with the Morgan-Guggenheim Syndicate whereby these lands would pass into the hands of the Syndicate. These complaints were investigated by Special Agents Love and Horace T. Jones, and L. R. Glavis who was to become Chief of the Field Division of the General Land Office, Portland, Oregon, in October 1907.

In the course of his investigations Glavis had become involved in a dispute with his superiors in the Department of the Interior, which eventually led him to seek the assistance of the Forest Service. He found evidence against the claimants showing that Cunningham as their agent had signed an option agreement with the Morgan-Guggenheim Syndicate on July 22, 1907. Glavis therefore objected to the clear listing of the Cunningham claims by Ballinger, who was then General Land Office Commissioner, and to what he considered attempts to prevent a thorough investigation of fraudulent practices. Two years later, after another General Land Office official, Special Agent James M. Sheridan, was put in charge of these investigations in June 1909, Glavis appealed for assistance to A. C. Shaw, Assistant Law Officer of the Forest Service at Portland, Oregon. This appeal to the Forest Service was made technically because the claims, if refused, would become a part of the Chugach National Forest. More important, however, in Glavis' mind was the possibility that the Forest Service might publicize the case to increase opposition to Ballinger's administration of the public lands.

In August 1909, while Pinchot was attending the Irrigation Congress at Spokane, Washington, Glavis turned to him and explained the Cunningham coal claims. Quickly grasping the political implications of Glavis' story, the Chief Forester furnished him with a personal letter of introduction to President Taft. Assisted by Shaw of the Forest Service, Glavis prepared a formal statement on the coal cases and personally presented it to the President at Beverly, Massachusetts, on August 18. This report did not formulate any specific charges against Ballinger or other Interior Department officials but hinted that these officials had taken steps favorable to the Cunningham claimants at a time when they knew or had reason to believe that the claims were fraudulent. On August 22 the President informed Ballinger and others involved as to Glavis' virtual accusation of bad faith on their part and requested them to make full replies.

Accordingly, on September 6, Ballinger, accompanied by Oscar W.

Lawler, an Assistant Attorney General especially assigned to the Interior Department, and armed with relevant supporting records, went to see the President at Beverly. Taft conferred with Ballinger, Lawler, and Attorney General Wickersham and examined the records relating to the coal cases. A few days later he informed Ballinger that he had concluded from the evidence presented that the contentions of Glavis embraced only shreds of suspicion without any substantial proof to sustain them. By this token he was clearly guilty of insubordination and Ballinger was authorized to dismiss him from government service. Taft brushed off lightly the fact that Ballinger had acted as attorney for the Cunningham claimants after having served the government as Commissioner of the General Land Office in the same cases. Said he to Ballinger: "I find the fact to be, that, as Commissioner, you acquired no knowledge in respect to the claims except that of the most formal character." [19]

The dismissal of Glavis and President Taft's exoneration of Ballinger and his assistants might have ended this dispute over the Alaskan coal lands, if only Pinchot could have been placated. Taft felt that it was necessary not only to keep Pinchot in the administration but at the same time to keep him out of quarrels with Ballinger. Thus writing his famous "My dear Gifford" letter under the same date as his public exoneration of Ballinger, September 13, he stated:

> I urge that you do not make Glavis's case yours. . . . I write this letter in order to prevent hasty action on your part in taking up Glavis's cause, or in objecting to my sustaining Ballinger and his subordinates within the Interior Department, as a reason for your withdrawing from the public service. I should consider it one of the greatest losses my administration could sustain if you were to leave it.
>
> I must bring public discussion between the two departments to an end. It is most demoralizing and subversive of governmental discipline and efficiency. I want you to help me in this.[20]

The President had earlier given this same impression in a conference with Professor Irving Fisher of Yale on September 3, 1909, after which the latter informed Pinchot that Taft appreciated him but was determined that he should not "wash the cabinet's dirty linen in public, or rather make it appear that there is dirty linen." [21]

---

[19] *Interior and Forestry Investigation*, VIII, 4508.
[20] Taft to Pinchot, September 13, 1909, GPP.
[21] Fisher to Pinchot, September 6, 1909, GPP.

Pinchot, however, was not appeased by the President's cordial gestures. Ballinger's acts and the President's approval of them rankled deeply. Granting that Ballinger might not have been actively hostile to conservation, which he was not fully prepared to concede, he felt still that was not enough for a man charged with the responsibilities of the Secretary of the Interior. Unless it could be proved that he was actively friendly, it went without saying, maintained Pinchot, that such a man was unfit for this office.[22] He was strengthened in his conviction by sentiments voiced by many prominent persons throughout the country. Henry C. Wallace, who at the time was a publisher of *Wallace's Farmer Post*, had written from Iowa:

> I feel it in my bones that Taft has gone over to the other side; and if for any reason this controversy should lead to your removal, or the resignation of Secretary Wilson, there will be black trouble ahead for the Taft administration.
>
> You have made a grand fight. . . . I am sure that the sentiment in this part of the country is with you.[23]

Expressing the strongest kind of support was Emerson Hough, the popular writer, who said that he and many of his friends stood squarely behind Pinchot because they believed he was right. But, right or wrong, they were with him.[24] Silas McBee, editor of the *Churchman*, wondered whether the supreme interests of the Nation, which demanded the most vigorous, aggressive, and positive action in the conservation policy, were likely to secure such action at the hands of a person like Ballinger. Criticizing the Taft-Ballinger strict interpretation of executive authority he asserted that "the difference between doing what the law specifically directs and what under the Constitution the Chief Executive as the representative of the people may do, without violating the law, is the difference between a stagnant administration and a living one."[25] By September 1909, Sir Horace Plunkett, the noted Irish agricultural reformer and frequent visitor to the United States, was becoming convinced that the Ballinger-Pinchot struggle was one between "the public good and monopoly."[26] Also among the Chief Forester's staunch supporters was the noted educator, David Starr Jordan, who declared: "I do not sympathize with the idea that the

---

[22] Pinchot to John H. Hammond, October 14, 1909, GPP.
[23] Wallace to Pinchot, August 17, 1909, GPP.
[24] Hough to Pinchot, September 17, 1909, GPP.
[25] Silas McBee, in *The Churchman*, October 9, 1909.
[26] Plunkett to Harry Hill, September 29, 1909, GPP.

Executive must be always 'fully buttressed within the law.' It is the men who are carrying off public property who should be 'fully buttressed' and the Executive should be on the firing line guarding the public interests on every quarter." [27]

By the close of 1909 the breach between Pinchot and the Taft administration was nearly complete. In December the Chief Forester set forth his grievances in a long letter to former President Roosevelt who was then on a hunting expedition in Africa. He accused Taft of surrounding himself with "a circle of trust attorneys and other reactionaries" who were "necessarily in opposition to the Roosevelt policies." The President had allowed attacks on "T. R." to continue in Congress unchecked when he might have ended them by speaking out, and had surrendered to Congress in its attack upon the Executive's power to appoint advisory commissions and thereby permitted the work of the National Conservation Commission to be stopped. Pinchot further complained that Taft had affiliated himself with and sought advice from anti-Roosevelt Congressional leaders like Cannon, Aldrich, Hale, Tawney, and others and had brought a dangerous attack on conservation by his appointment of Ballinger. At the same time he had attempted to read out of the party Senators Nelson, Beveridge, Cummins, and other fighters for the "square deal." The principle of federal regulation and control over waterpower on navigable streams had been impaired if not abandoned. Finally the President was alleged to have placed himself in a position where his only alliance was with "special interests" and thereby to have allowed the great majority of the American people to lose confidence in his administration.[28]

Meanwhile added to this persistent criticism of the Taft-Ballinger position had been the publication of Glavis' story of the Alaskan coal cases. Following his dismissal from the General Land Office, Glavis, with the knowledge of Shaw and Price of the Forest Service, had written to the President asserting that "since there now may be greater danger that these coal lands will be fraudulently secured by the Syndicate, it is no less duty to my country to make public these facts in my possession concerning which I firmly believe you have been misled." [29] After Shaw and Price had examined his manuscript, Glavis published his story in the November 13, 1909, issue of *Collier's Weekly* under the title "The Whitewashing of Ballinger — Are the

[27] Jordan to Pinchot, October 19, 1909, GPP.
[28] Pinchot to Roosevelt, December 31, 1909, GPP.
[29] *Interior and Forestry Investigation*, IV, 888.

Guggenheims in Charge of the Department of Interior?" The article, based in part upon information supplied from official Forest Service files by Shaw and Price, together with the previous anti-Ballinger agitation, provoked demands for a Congressional investigation of the Interior Department and Forest Service.

In accordance with a request from Senator J. P. Dolliver, Chairman of the Senate Committee on Agriculture, Pinchot wrote a letter to the Senator concerning the conduct of Shaw and Price. There was no definite agreement, but the Chief Forester had the impression that his superior, Secretary of Agriculture James Wilson, had no objection to his answering Senator Dolliver's request. Thus, on January 6, 1910, the same day on which President Taft transmitted documents that contained the bases for his conclusions exonerating Ballinger, Pinchot's letter was read in the Senate. Pinchot acknowledged that his subordinate officials, Shaw and Price, had made public certain official information concerning the Cunningham coal claims and had approved the publication by Glavis of certain facts concerning these claims after he was no longer in government service. He conceded that these officials had violated a rule of propriety as between federal departments, and stated that they had received an official reprimand. At the same time, he recommended without hesitation that no further action be taken in their case and added that "measured by the emergency which forced them, by the purity of their motives, and the results which they accomplished, their breach of propriety sinks well nigh into insignificance." [30]

This defiant attitude of the Chief Forester thoroughly exasperated President Taft. Consequently, in a letter of January 7, 1910, he took the fateful step of informing Pinchot that Secretary Wilson was directed to remove him from office. In his letter the President pointed out that Price had offered to resign on the ground that he had been engaged with Shaw in instigating the publication of various material attacking the good name of Secretary Ballinger and charging the Interior Department with corruption. He indicated that Secretary Wilson had asked for Pinchot's recommendation concerning this matter and the latter had stated that he wished to make a statement to be read in the Senate at the same time that the President's message transmitting the Glavis case records reached there, and that Pinchot had written a statement to Senator Dolliver against the advice of Secretary Wilson,

[30] Pinchot to Dolliver, January 5, 1910, *Congressional Record*, January 6, 1910, p. 378.

his superior.[31] Commenting on this statement the President declared that

> the plain intimations in your letter are, first, that, I had reached
> a wrong conclusion as to the good faith of Secretary Ballinger
> and the officers of the Land Office, although you and your sub-
> ordinates had only seen or read the evidence of Glavis, the
> accuser, and had never seen or read the evidence of those ac-
> cused . . . and second, that, under the circumstances, without
> the exploitation by Messrs. Shaw and Price in the . . . press of
> the charges of Glavis, the administration including the President
> and the law officers of the Interior Department and Land Office,
> would have allowed certain fraudulent claims to be patented on
> coal lands in Alaska, although the matter had been specifically
> brought to the attention of the President by the Glavis charges.

Taft concluded significantly: "By your own conduct you have destroyed your usefulness as a helpful subordinate of the Government,
and it therefore becomes my duty to direct the Secretary of Agriculture
to remove you from your office as The Forester." [32]

This action by President Taft could hardly have surprised Pinchot
or any close observer of the Ballinger-Pinchot dispute. The Chief
Forester had actually courted dismissal to emphasize and perhaps even
to dramatize his disagreement with the Taft administration in a cause
for which he had been acknowledge to be the guiding spirit. When
dismissal came, he was jubilant rather than downcast. Officials of the
Forest Service in Washington who assembled on January 8 when their
chief bade them good-bye, did not forget his confidence that right,
as he saw it, would eventually triumph, nor his exhortation that the
Service must carry on the fight for conservation.

There was mixed reaction to Pinchot's departure from the Forest
Service. The unhappiness of subordinate officers and other personnel
of the Service was only partially diminished by Taft's selection of

---

[31] Immediately after Pinchot's letter to Senator Dolliver had been read in the
Senate, Senator Hale had said that it was a breach of Taft's executive order issued
on November 29, 1909, forbidding a subordinate official to give information to a
member of Congress or a committee without the consent of the head of the department. Pinchot had discussed this order with Secretary Wilson and according
to the latter's own statement before the Congressional investigating committee on
March 1910, he had made no objection. Wilson, however, apparently did not see
the letter to Dolliver until it had been read in the Senate and did not think
that Pinchot would state that the President had been misinformed about the
Glavis case.

[32] Personnel file of Pinchot, RG 16.

Henry S. Graves, a friend and former associate, to be the new head of the Service. Secretary Wilson, in contrast, was obviously relieved, for he confided to B. T. Galloway, Chief of the Bureau of Plant Industry, that the "Pinchot matter was most unfortunate" but he had been "begging him all summer to take another course."[33] A few days later he chided Pinchot for acting as though he had been "ordained" to do forestry work and complained to Galloway: "The Lord knows every step that he took that was of value was ordered by myself, and much that I wanted done with regard to planting trees, etc. he has not done."[34] On the other hand, former President Roosevelt declared that the "blow" of Pinchot's dismissal was not lightened by the appointment of a "man of high character, a noted forestry expert" in his place, for he considered the deposed Forester to have been the "leader among all men in public office — and the aggressive hard-hitting leader — of all the forces . . . struggling for conservation and . . . fighting for the general interest as against special privilege."[35]

The Republican majority of a Congressional committee appointed to investigate the Ballinger-Pinchot controversy (or more technically, the Interior Department and the Forest Service) upheld Ballinger's position. It reported in December 1910 that "neither any act proved nor all facts put together exhibit Mr. Ballinger as anything but a competent and honorable gentlemen, earnestly and faithfully performing the duties of high office with an eye to the public interest."[36] Earlier the Democratic minority of the investigating committee upheld Pinchot's contentions. It reported that "Richard A. Ballinger has not been true to the trust reposed in him as Secretary of the Interior, that he is not deserving of public confidence, and that he should be requested by the proper authorities to resign his office."[37] An insurgent Republican member of the committee substantially agreed with the minority and recommended that he should not be retained in office, since he apparently was no friend of conservation.[38]

No action was taken by Congress upon either the majority or minority reports. *Collier's Weekly* which had vigorously championed the position of Pinchot and Glavis, with the most damaging sort of accusations and insinuations against the integrity of Ballinger, was not sued, contrary

---

[33] Wilson to Galloway, January 20, 1910, Letters Sent, RG 16.
[34] Wilson to Galloway, February 12, 1910, Letters Sent, RG 16.
[35] Roosevelt to Pinchot, March 1, 1910, GPP.
[36] *Interior and Forestry Investigation*, I, 90.
[37] *Interior and Forestry Investigation*, I, 147.
[38] *Interior and Forestry Investigation*, I, 192.

to many expectations. The Cunningham claims were cancelled. Most of the nation's press continued to demand Ballinger's dismissal despite his exoneration by the Republican majority and doubtless contributed to the election of a Democratic majority to the House of Representatives in 1910.

President Taft was unable to banish the rising storm of popular protest, yet reluctant to retreat from his defense of his unpopular Secretary of the Interior. Muckraking periodicals inquired why the President did not dismiss Ballinger. "Is he afraid of him and the money interests that support him?" they asked. Finally the discredited Secretary relieved the President's embarrassment by resigning from the cabinet in March 1911.

In the light of subsequent study of the evidence in the Ballinger-Pinchot controversy, the partisan reports of the Congressional investigating committee seem inconclusive as to Ballinger's active complicity in the Alaska coal-land claims. The controversy did not necessarily imply any great moral obliquity on the part of either Ballinger or Pinchot. In the records of the case the worst that was imputed to the Secretary of the Interior was a serious lack of the sense of propriety in pleading the case of his clients, the Cunningham interests, as against the General Land Office, in which he had but recently been employed as an official. A somewhat analogous case would be that of a lawyer who had been employed in a certain case by the defendant and after becoming familiar with the facts under litigation should withdraw and accept a retainer for the plaintiff. The real question hinged on policy and legal interpretation. The Ballinger policy was one of immediate development of natural resources in the absence of specific restraining legislation and at the possible risk of allowing control of these resources to fall into the hands of predatory interests. The Pinchot policy was one of protecting the public resources from monopolistic interests by liberal interpretation of existing legislation and at the possible risk of delaying the development of the resources.

Heated accusations by Pinchot and other conservationists obscured the fact that Ballinger under Taft's direction actually expanded certain phases of the conservation program initiated by Roosevelt and Pinchot. This was especially true with respect to the withdrawal of public mineral lands. Surpassing Roosevelt's action in this connection, President Taft on September 26, 1909, withdrew from all forms of entry 2,871,000 acres of petroleum land in California and 170,000 acres in Wyoming. Roosevlt had withdrawn only from agricultural entry the Wyoming land and 2,270,044 acres of the California land. As early as

February 1908 George O. Smith, Director of the Geological Survey had suggested to Secretary Garfield the desirability of making more absolute withdrawals to conserve petroleum resources for the Navy. However, no action was taken until Smith discussed the matter with Secretary Ballinger.[39]

Despite the Roosevelt administration's attack on the monopolistic practices of the Standard Oil Company, it seems to have been less concerned over the possible fraudulent acquisition of oil land than of other resources of the public domain. Prior to July 1, 1909, gross oil land withdrawals covered only about four million acres as compared with forty-two million acres of coal lands. In addition to withdrawals of oil land which President Taft authorized in September 1909, between then and June 30, 1910, he authorized thirteen new withdrawals extending over nearly three million acres.[40]

Ballinger's action was defended in recent years by the late former Secretary of the Interior Harold Ickes, who contended that Ballinger was an "innocent victim" of public wrath aroused by Pinchot. Ickes declared:

> It is a fair conclusion that the press, and particularly the public, would have accepted Taft's exoneration of Ballinger had not the Forest Service, under the leadership of Pinchot, kept the controversy alive by inducing Glavis to write his article for Collier's Weekly and by supplying sensational material to muckraking publications which could be used to reflect upon Ballinger and, inferentially, upon President Taft.[41]

Ickes, however, who was bitter against Pinchot because of the latter's opposition in the 1930's to his plan to make Interior a "Department of Conservation" with control over the national forests, overstated his case with the assertion that "the congressional investigating committee completely exonerated Ballinger."[42] Actually, of course, only seven of the twelve committee members exonerated Ballinger. Furthermore, Ickes failed to point out that the majority report, while exonerating Ballinger, declared in favor of retention of coal lands in public ownership, enactment of legislation providing for the leasing of coal lands, and continuation of the then-existing withdrawal of lands from entry

[39] John Ise, *The United States Oil Policy* (New Haven, 1926), pp. 312–313.
[40] Ise, *Oil Policy*, p. 313.
[41] Ickes, *Not Guilty*, p. 47.
[42] Ickes, p. 46.

pending enactment of such legislation. These measures in essence were courses advocated by Pinchot and Glavis.

Pinchot's role in this controversy certainly was not without vindictiveness and was calculated to dramatize the dispute in favor of his own notion of conservation. His fall from grace as a presidential adviser was no doubt a bitter draught to add to his disappointment over Taft's failure to reappoint Garfield. It is probable also that much of his attack directly upon Ballinger and indirectly upon Taft was prompted by political considerations. Throughout the dispute and long after his dismissal he spoke and wrote more as a politician than as a scientific expert. Nevertheless, the fact remains that in his opposition to a policy that had led to monopoly and deprived the public of valuable resources without adequate consideration in remuneration or service, Pinchot exhibited unusual foresight and social understanding that were abundantly confirmed by subsequent events. The publicity and dramatization that he gave to the controversy went far toward more firmly establishing conservation as a federal administrative program and a matter of fundamental public policy.

XVI

Continuing Forest Interests

$\mathbf{F}$OR A DECADE after his dismissal from the Forest Service, Pinchot's interest and activities were centered mainly in national and state politics which seemed to take him irrevocably away from forestry. During these years he was an unsuccessful candidate for U.S. Senator from Pennsylvania and a leading spokesman for the Progressive Party. Occasionally, his political hopes may have extended even to the White House. Alpheus T. Mason, who defended Pinchot's role in the celebrated controversy, observes that thirty editors polled by the *Chicago Tribune* voted for him as a possible presidential candidate for 1912.[1] Pinchot's ambitious political objectives of this period thus have tended to obscure his less pretentious but not insignificant continuing interest in forestry, which now to a greater degree was focused at a state level. He was nonetheless still guided by the same goals and principles that had been basic to his achievements in the federal Forest Service.

That Pinchot had not altogether relinquished his concern for forestry on the national level was evident in activities of the National Conservation Association, which he had organized in the summer of 1909 and generously supported with personal funds. In large part, the Association was the outgrowth of Pinchot's displeasure with the Congressional

---

[1] Alpheus T. Mason, *Bureaucracy Convicts Itself*, p. 90. For a good account of Pinchot's political activities during these years, see McGeary, *Gifford Pinchot*, pp. 190–272; and Fausold, *Gifford Pinchot*.

action that had ended the work of the National Conservation Commission earlier that same year, and his feeling that a strong pressure group was urgently needed to provide continuing assistance in the fight for conservation.[2] His hope that the American Forestry Association might logically provide such assistance had vanished by 1909 when that organization shifted from a broad conservation program emphasizing federal responsibilities to one limited mainly to forest conservation with stress on the responsibilities of states and private forest owners.[3]

For his new National Conservation Association, then, Pinchot persuaded Charles W. Eliot, outgoing president of Harvard University, to serve as the Association's president, and James R. Garfield and Henry L. Stimson to serve on its board of directors. Staff work of the Association at various intervals was entrusted largely to able publicists and close associates of Pinchot such as Thomas R. Shipp, Harry Slattery, Overton Price, Philip P. Wells, and George Woodruff. Although its activities were considerably tinged with politics, the Association could not be accused of working only for the political advancement of its founder.[4] Among its principal efforts were a campaign to prevent transfer of control over national forests to the states and work for legislation to control the development of waterpower on federal government property.[5] The issues of waterpower and forest policy were often joined, because during this period it was estimated that a great part of the waterpower capable of development in the United States was within the boundaries of national forests.[6]

State control over the national forests was sought by powerful western interests in a continuing thrust against increased federal regulation of forest uses anathematized with the term "Pinchotism." After 1910, bills seeking state control of the national forests were repeatedly introduced in Congress. By 1913 Pinchot, then president and clearly the dominant force in the National Conservation Association, characterized the supporters of these bills as "grabbers of natural resources" who were "getting mighty hungry" and were determined to fight a national conservation policy.[7] His effective opposition contributed to the defeat

---

[2] J. Leonard Bates, "Fulfilling American Democracy: The Conservation Movement, 1907 to 1921," *Mississippi Valley Historical Review*, XLIV (June 1957), 36.
[3] Hays, *Conservation and the Gospel of Efficiency*, pp. 179–180.
[4] McGeary, *Gifford Pinchot*, pp. 200–201.
[5] McGeary, p. 203.
[6] Cameron, *Development of Governmental Forest Control in the United States*, p. 300.
[7] Pinchot, quoted in *American Lumberman*, January 18, 1913.

of this proposed legislation. On the waterpower issue he was ardently assisted by Woodruff and Wells who worked with him to establish broader application of the policy, originating with the Forest Service, that waterpower sites owned by the federal government should not be sold or leased in perpetuity and that the government should maintain sufficient control over power development on the sites to protect the public interest and prevent excessive private profit. This effort was to be ultimately rewarded to a considerable degree by passage of the Water Power Act of 1920 establishing broadly the principle of federal regulation of hydroelectric power.

In addition to directing the work of the National Conservation Association in the decade after 1910, Pinchot wrote numerous articles related to forestry for leading periodicals, collected data for a proposed history of the American forest movement (to be noted later), and spoke to varied groups concerned with forest questions. Of special interest in the history of American forest policy was the advice he gave to Franklin D. Roosevelt, who in 1912 in the New York State Senate was attempting to develop an effective forest protection program for the state. At Roosevelt's request, Pinchot gave an illustrated talk on the Adirondack forest situation in the New York State Assembly chamber on February 20, 1912, and helped him to frame a bill for "Protection of Lands, Forests, and Public Parks" in New York.[8] His contact with Pinchot during this legislative experience Roosevelt regarded as the beginning of his own thinking about conservation.

Along with his continuing interest in matters of national forest policy during this time, Pinchot became increasingly concerned about forest policy in Pennsylvania. Dating back to 1897, and under the guidance of Dr. J. T. Rothrock, Pinchot's early mentor and the state's first Commissioner of Forestry, the notable progress toward forest protection in Pennsylvania had been mainly attributable to state acquisition and administration of forest lands. A primary objective had been management under forestry principles for timber production.[9] The program had reached a high-water mark between 1902 and 1909 with the acquisition of more than 500,000 acres.[10] By 1913 Pennsylvania had become

---

[8] Rexford G. Tugwell, *The Democratic Roosevelt* (Garden City, 1957), pp. 82–83. Pinchot's diary, February 20, 1912, GPP.

[9] Smith, Tillotson, and O'Donnell, *National Plan for American Forestry* (73d Cong., 1st Sess.), I, 763.

[10] Report titled, "A Short Statement About Pennsylvania Forestry," 1922, Research Compilation File, RG 95.

a "timber land millionaire" with holdings of 1,000,681 acres, and was second only to New York among the leading state owners of forests.[11]

Notwithstanding the progress, Pinchot became convinced that Pennsylvania's forest program was unsatisfactory. To strengthen his political ties with farmers, he had joined the Pennsylvania State Grange; and by 1918, as chairman of its conservation committee, he could openly express his opinion of the state's forestry situation. His impressions were apparently strengthened by an inspection in November 1918 of several state forest areas, including Mount Alto, Bald Eagle, Oleona, Austin, Pine Creek, Jersey Shore, and Bellefonte.[12] Shortly after his tour he complained that the State Department of Forestry was defective in several respects, and that the office of State Commissioner of Forestry, then held by Robert S. Conklin, should be in the hands of a technically trained forester. Also under criticism were Conklin's tendency to concern himself with details of local forest management that he should have entrusted to subordinate officers, the lack of a uniform system of accounting for the various forests, the absence of an inspection system, and inadequacies in fire control facilities, forest personnel, and funds for purchase of forest lands.[13]

Conklin, who had been Commissioner since 1904, seemed surprised by Pinchot's criticism, but did not ignore it. He replied that the state forests were being managed by trained foresters in accordance with "principles of scientific and practical forestry" and were being developed "just so rapidly and so far as the Legislature permits." He acknowledged the state's need for many observation towers, telephone lines, fire fighters, and fire-fighting instruments, but maintained that his Department, despite disadvantages, had been successful in reducing substantially the average area burned per fire each year. He added: "This Department is organized for business and not for show."[14]

Not satisfied by Conklin's presentation of facts, Pinchot pursued his subject further. To buttress his view of Pennsylvania's specific needs, in March 1919 he sent a letter to the chief of the U.S. Forest Service and heads of state forest agencies, asking their opinion as to the wisdom of employing state foresters with or without technical training.

---

[11] Report of Forest Inspector George H. Wirt in Philadelphia *North American*, January 25, 1914.

[12] Report on itinerary of Pinchot, November 1918, GPP.

[13] Report of the Pennsylvania State Grange Committee on Conservation, December 11, 1918, GPP.

[14] Statement titled, "Facts Relating to the Pennsylvania State Forests," February 14, 1919, GPP.

He was gratified that most responses favored appointment of trained men whenever possible, as did Henry Graves of the Forest Service in his reply: "Taking the country over, progress in putting State forestry on a sound basis has been almost absolutely dependent on the placing of technically trained and practically experienced men in the positions of State foresters. . . . The Forest Service has always urged the fundamental importance of placing trained foresters at the head of State forest organizations."[15]

Conklin, on the other hand, was not without some supporters who thought Pinchot's criticism was unjustly harsh. Frank W. Rane, State Forester of Massachusetts, for example, expressed high regard for the Forestry Department's educational and research work at the Mont Alto Forest Academy and stated that during World War I, Academy personnel gave valuable technical assistance to his state in its wood utilization program.[16]

Governor William C. Sproul of Pennsylvania apparently felt that criticism of his state's forest work by the nation's outstanding forester and a politically ambitious Pennsylvanian could not be taken lightly. Hence, in August 1919, he prevailed on Pinchot to serve on the Pennsylvania Forest Commission, the state's forest-policy-making body. The closer perspective afforded him as a Commission member reinforced Pinchot's opinion that the state's forest organization and methods needed considerable overhauling. Thus, with characteristic vigor, he pressed his criticism of Conklin at a Commission meeting in October. Here he introduced motions requesting the Forestry Commissioner to present to the Forest Commission for its examination existing plans for fire protection in each State forest district; revised rules and regulations relating to the care, use, and protection of State forests and transaction of business thereon; standard forms for contracts for timber sales, grazing, mineral leases, ground leases, and other uses of State forests; a plan for the reduction or relocation of nurseries as might be required by more emphasis on fire protection measures; a plan for consolidation of State forests into units capable of being administered by one man; and a plan for systematic inspection of State forests. He also moved that the chief forest warden be instructed to take necessary steps to secure from private timberland owners their compliance with an act of 1915 relating to conditions contributing to forest fire hazards, that the Commission consider plans for acquisition of additional State

---

[15] Graves to Pinchot, March 10, 1919, GPP.
[16] Rane to Pinchot, March 18, 1919, GPP.

forest land on the Ohio Watershed, and that future timber sales on State forests be made only on direct authority of the Forest Commission. These motions suggesting displeasure, if not a lack of confidence, in Conklin's administration were approved by the Commission.[17]

Pinchot was not alone in his criticism of the state forest work. Within the same month, he persuaded a colleague, Henry W. Shoemaker, to join him in signing a sixteen-page statement denouncing the management of the state's forest and sharply criticizing the organization of the Department of Forestry.[18] And Rothrock, venerable conservationist and a fellow member of the Forest Commission, expressed dissatisfaction with conditions in a state forest in Potter County. After an October visit to this site, he had called attention to the need for eliminating fire-scarred trees with "careful lumbering" to encourage natural regeneration and urged that the remaining timber of the forest be sold under provisions for advertising and competitive bidding and possibly with the use of revised contract forms.[19]

Criticism of Conklin's administration continued at meetings of the Commission during November and December 1919. Pinchot influenced the Commission to direct that Conklin submit a budget for each forest, and that the chief forest fire warden determine whether conditions on the forest lands of lumber companies in Pennsylvania constituted a public nuisance within the meaning of the forest act of 1915. He also obtained approval of his recommendation that the Commission consider acquisition of additional forest lands in areas of the state containing few state forests, especially the area on the Ohio Watershed.[20] Moreover, knowing from his administration of the federal Forest Service the effectiveness of publicity, he had tried to have meetings of the Forest Commission held open to the public. His Commission colleagues, however, were hesitant to take this action without consultation with Governor Sproul.[21] Meanwhile, the State Grange Conservation Committee was serving as a medium for his attack. In a report (undoubtedly written by Pinchot) released in December 1919, this Committee characterized the Forest Commission as a "closed corporation," criticized Conklin's handling of timber sales and fire control work,

[17] Minutes of the Forest Commission, October 14, 1919, GPP.
[18] Pinchot and Shoemaker to Sproul, October 13, 1919, GPP.
[19] Rothrock to Conklin, November 3, 1919, GPP.
[20] Minutes of the Forest Commission, November 7, 1919, and December 12, 1919, GPP.
[21] Minutes of the Forest Commission, December 12, 1919.

and concluded that the state forests were "not safe in his hands" and would not be safe until he was removed.[22]

By the end of the year, Governor Sproul sensed that this feud over forestry in his administration would have to be ended. Accordingly, he suggested that objective experts from outside Pennsylvania be employed to review the arguments. The proposal, not surprisingly, was entirely unsatisfactory to Pinchot who let it be known that he "did not recognize that anyone in America had a right to pass upon [his] opinion as a Forester."[23] The Governor apparently was not inclined to challenge this retort and consequently decided to replace Conklin. The matter was facilitated by Conklin's resignation, and he later accepted a position with the State Board of Water Supply.

Early in 1920 Sproul expressed interest in having Pinchot as the Commissioner of Forestry, although the latter appeared to be reluctant to accept the position, possibly for fear of seeming to be losing his political independence. But in March 1920, when he received a formal request from Sproul to accept appointment as Commissioner, he agreed to serve.[24] Obviously pleased with this turn of events, the Governor announced: "I have commandeered Mr. Pinchot's services. We have in him a citizen, who is the foremost figure in forestry in the United States, and I thought we should have the benefit of his services at home. Mr. Pinchot has been used to handling national problems but Pennsylvania is an empire itself."[25] Pinchot explained that he had answered the call of the Governor to help him accomplish "one of the biggest things" that could be done for Pennsylvania, namely, to stop forest fires and put back into the productive area of the state some five or six million acres of unproductive land.[26]

Pinchot's appointment won enthusiastic approval by most Pennsylvanians and it was hailed as an important personal tribute by forest conservationists throughout the country. The suggestion that the appointment was a clever political conquest by the state's regular Republican organization was unacceptable to Philadelphia's influential newspaper, the *North American*.[27] But the Washington *Post* probably expressed the view of many observers of the fading fortunes of the

[22] Report of Pennsylvania State Grange Committee on Conservation, December 10, 1919, GPP.
[23] Pinchot to Shoemaker, December 23, 1919, GPP.
[24] Pinchot to Sproul, March 3, 1920, GPP.
[25] Philadelphia *Public Ledger*, March 11, 1920.
[26] Philadelphia *Public Ledger*, March 11, 1920.
[27] Philadelphia *North American*, April 10, 1920.

Progressive Party when it surmised that Pinchot had been "taken over body and breeches by the Old Guard" as represented by the Sproul administration.[28] There was no reason, however, to disagree with the observation of the American Forestry Association that forest conservationists throughout the United States applauded Pinchot's appointment as Pennsylvania's chief forester.[29]

---

[28] Washington (D.C.) *Post*, March 13, 1920.
[29] *American Forestry*, xxvi (March 1920), 177.

XVII

In Penn's Woods

As COMMISSIONER OF FORESTRY for Pennsylvania, Pinchot established an administration characterized by strong executive leadership, dynamic public relations, and diversified forest work that was remarkably reminiscent of his direction of the U.S. Forest Service. Once again he had some official and professional vantage ground from which he could effectively ponder and prod the progress of American forestry.

Shortly after he assumed office on March 10, 1920, the new Commissioner proceeded with a major reorganization of the Department of Forestry. To provide more effective fiscal control, he established a budget and accounting system for the Department as a whole and for each individual forest. The state was divided into twenty-four forest districts, each supervised by a trained forester charged with conducting an intensive campaign for the detection, prevention, and suppression of forest fires. Subordinate to the district forester were foresters in charge of particular forest sites, forest rangers, and other district employees. Each district was provided with a comprehensive fire plan designed to facilitate handling of its outstanding protection problems. A system of inspection was instituted to establish closer contact between the Commissioner's office in Harrisburg, the foresters in the field, and the public. The reorganized Department of Forestry now functioned through four Bureaus (Operation, Silviculture, Lands, and Forest Protection) and four Offices (Research, Information, Maintenance, and

State Forest Academy).[1] Throughout the whole Department, the organizational and functional pattern of the U.S. Forest Service was recognizable.

"Keeping the public well and correctly informed about forestry" was stated to be one of the principal functions of the reorganized Department of Forestry.[2] Hence Pinchot immediately launched what amounted to an extensive education program to publicize the aims and activities of the Department and to secure broader public support for protection and development of state forest lands. He emphasized the need to prevent destructive forest fires which, he contended, had made a desert in Pennsylvania larger than the whole State of New Jersey. He complained that Pennsylvania had appropriated for forest fire protection during a six-year period before 1920 less than $30,000 per year, or not a quarter of a cent per forest acre. This, he declared, was "like trying to put out a burning building with water in a spoon." [3] The plight of Pennsylvania forestry was the subject of the Commissioner's conferences with several business, professional, and civic groups. One of the most notable was a meeting with officials of all the state's principal railroads held at the State Capitol on May 4, 1920. These officials pledged their companies to burn or clear a safety strip, averaging 100 feet, on each side of their tracks and to comply with federal safety rules relating to spark arresters and ash pans.[4] With the substantial compliance that followed, the Department of Forestry was able to report two years later that the railroads had burned more than 1,560 miles of safety strips at a cost to them of $73,526.32 (nearly double the amount spent by the Department for fire extinction in any year). This was applauded as a "precedent in railroad forest protection cooperation unparalleled in the country." [5]

Another important conference in Harrisburg, April 13 and 14, 1921, brought together sixty-seven representatives of important wood-using industries in Pennsylvania. On this occasion the Commissioner described the state's worsening timber situation and discussed its timber needs. During the summers of 1920 and 1921, in meetings with state foresters at Mont Alto, all phases of the state's forest work were re-

---

[1] Pennsylvania Department of Forestry, *Report, 1920–1921* (Harrisburg, 1922), pp. 6–7 (cited hereafter as *Forestry Department Report, 1920–21*).
[2] *Forestry Department Report, 1920–21*, p. 19.
[3] Pinchot to Sproul, April 6, 1920, GPP.
[4] Notes of a conference with railroad officials, May 4, 1920, Fire Control Division Correspondence, RG 95.
[5] *Forestry Department Report, 1920–21*, p. 10.

viewed and plans were formulated for increasing its effectiveness. Along with efforts at the state level, Pinchot persevered in his larger mission to acquaint the public with forestry conditions affecting the nation in general. State and federal foresters convened in Harrisburg on December 8 and 9, 1920, to pursue the problem. Still other conferences were held and, in addition, Forestry Department personnel spoke before numerous business and civic organizations and wrote hundreds of newspaper articles on the subject. Popular talks by Pinchot emphasizing the economic value of forests were given wide circulation in a Department bulletin.[6] An exhibit on forest conditions in Pennsylvania and activities of the Forestry Department was prepared and displayed at five country teachers institutes, one farm products show, twelve county fairs, one road celebration, one forester's meeting, and one flower show. Scarcely any gathering was ignored in the Department's program of "public education."[7]

Effectively supplementing the official publicity was the work of a private group known as the Committee on the Restoration of Pennsylvania's Timber Production, which had been organized during the summer of 1920. Sponsored and advised mainly by Pinchot, the Committee had as its principal officers Louis C. Madeira III (Chairman), a Philadelphia business leader; Mrs. Frank B. Black (Vice-Chairman), Director of the State Federation of Pennsylvania Women; A. Nevin Detrich (Secretary), member of the State Grange Conservation Committee; and George E. Lippincott (Treasurer), Chairman of the Forestry Committee of the Philadelphia Wholesale Lumber Dealers' Association. The Committee's principal aims were to secure a state appropriation of one million dollars for fire protection for two years, a larger appropriation for administration of the Department of Forestry, and five million dollars for the purchase of more lands for state forest purposes. It also vigorously supported a plan for amendment of the state constitution to permit issuance of bonds up to 25 million dollars for the purchase of forest lands. The Committee had the support of some thirty leading business, civic, and conservation organizations in Pennsylvania and by January 1921 had been able to hold meetings on the forest problem in each of Pennsylvania's sixty-seven counties. Declaring that what Pennsylvania was doing in awakening its people to the importance of forest restoration could be done by other states, the Committee observed: "All that is necessary is to get the bare facts be-

---

[6] Pinchot, *Talks on Forestry* (Pa. Dept. of Forestry Bulletin 32, 1923).
[7] *See Forestry Department Report, 1920–21,* p. 20.

fore the people, and especially the business people. Public sentiment will do the rest."[8] The message of the Committee had been reaching churches and synagogues as well as business clubs and civic forums. At the suggestion of the Committee, November 21, 1920, had been proclaimed as "Forest Protection Sunday" and the Sabbath immediately preceding Thanksgiving Day as a "Forest Protection" day. These special days were used to advise Pennsylvanians of the "real facts" concerning their forests and to help educate them as to the "importance of putting an end to forest fires and forest devastation and to restoring Penn's Woods."[9]

The vigor with which Pinchot moved to reorganize and publicize Pennsylvania's forest program was matched by energetic and often innovative effort in forest administration and research, in which detection, prevention, and suppression of forest fires constituted an important part. In this connection he established a fire control organization rated by the U.S. Forest Service as the best state organization of its kind. Employed in this program were some 2,600 salaried and per diem workers, nearly twice as many as were employed in any year prior to 1920, and they received special training and improved equipment for detection and fighting of forest fires.[10] The program was greatly facilitated by the erection of some fifty steel observation towers with telephone linkage to headquarters of the district foresters, forest rangers, and other leading fire fighters.[11] A further contribution to the effort was the increased cooperation of railroads in building safety strips, using other preventive measures, and extinguishing fires. Thanks to this cooperation the area of the average forest fire was reduced, although the number of fires caused by the railroads increased as the amount of traffic became greater. Construction of nearly 500 miles of forest roads and trails and the repair of some 2,500 miles of roads and trails provided additional protection.[12]

Next in priority in the Pinchot administration was an accelerated land acquisition program, under which 77,544 acres of forest lands were purchased by the state at an average cost of $2.00 per acre.[13]

[8] Statement concerning the Committee on the Restoration of Pennsylvania's Timber Production prepared in January 1921, GPP.

[9] Form letter of the committee to ministers, November 8, 1920, GPP.

[10] *Forestry Department Report, 1920–21*, pp. 8–9.

[11] George H. Wirt to Louis S. Murphy, January 31, 1922, Cooperative Forest Protection Division Correspondence, RG 95.

[12] *Forestry Department Report, 1920–21*, p. 11.

[13] *Forestry Department Report, 1920–21*, pp. 12–13.

Land purchases for the preceding two-year period of the Conklin administration had mounted to only 30,919 acres and had cost an average of $2.26 per acre.[14] During 1921 the Department of Forestry made a survey of forest land available for state purchase and received purchase offers for approximately 750,000 acres. It was unable to take advantage of these offers, however, because Governor Sproul disapproved of the expenditure of $500,000 for acquisition purposes. The setback doubtless spurred Pinchot's determination to obtain a State bond issue of 25 million dollars for the purchase of about 3,500,000 acres of nonproductive forest land. This purchase, it was maintained, was needed to insure "future citizens of the State against timber want and to bequeath to them a timber heritage necessary for their prosperity."[15] Despite his energetic publicity campaign, Pinchot as a forester and later as governor (1923–27, 1931–35) was unable to get a constitutional amendment authorizing the bond issue.[16]

Concurrently with his other conservation endeavors, Pinchot's administrative prowess was also evident in an expanded program of cooperation with private timberland owners and state agencies. Again drawing on his earlier experience in the U.S. Forest Service, he provided Department of Forestry personnel for free examination of private tracts of timberland of less than 200 acres and for examination of larger tracts at a cost to owners of only the actual expenses incurred by personnel. The examining foresters were also directed to prepare reports to the owners with recommendations for improved forest management practices.[17] Beginning in July 1920, Pinchot's assistants examined some 28,659 acres on 131 tracts.[18] The distribution of forest tree seedlings to private forest owners, a service begun in 1910 by the Department of Forestry, was an important stimulus to expanding private reforestation efforts. During 1921 alone, some three million seedlings were distributed. This was reported to be an increase of 4,447 per cent over the number distributed in 1912.[19]

Another facet of Pinchot's Department of Forestry activities was a cooperative program with the State Highway Department. Highway

[14] *Report of the Forestry Department, 1918–19*, p. 7.

[15] Pennsylvania Department of Forests and Waters, *Report, 1922–1924* (Harrisburg, 1924), p. 7.

[16] McGeary, *Gifford Pinchot*, p. 330.

[17] Statement titled, "Policy of Cooperation with Timberland Owners," 1920, GPP.

[18] *Forestry Department Report*, 1920–21, p. 15.

[19] *Forestry Department Report*, 1920–21, p. 14.

plantings in 1921 totaled more than 5,000 trees furnished from nurseries of the Department of Forestry, which staked out their location along highways, directed the planting operations and provided supervision for pruning and treatment against insect and fungus attacks.[20] To help meet the demands for trees in this highway beautification program and the distribution program for private planting, the Department of Forestry in 1921 arranged for the establishment of twelve cooperative tree nurseries at various state institutions to supplement the production of four Departmental nurseries.[21] Also included in the joint effort were plans for extensive participation of Boy Scout and Girl Scout organizations in forest fire control work and for continued forest protection activities in conjunction with the U.S. Forest Service under the Weeks Act, and combined fire observation measures with the State of Maryland along the Mason-Dixon line.

Though obscured by dramatic activities on behalf of forest protection and acquisition, Pinchot's endeavors for forest research and education strengthened Pennsylvania's forest program. He recognized that a forest crop, like any agricultural crop, was susceptible of intensive management. Thus he saw the need for more scientific knowledge concerning the state's trees and their qualities for production and utilization. To this end, he authorized a number of special research projects dealing with such subjects as forest reproduction, conversion, and growth; timber supply; and wood-using industries.[22] To obtain more reliable data concerning forest growth and yield he approved the establishment of fifty-seven sample plots on public and private forest lands — another practice borrowed from his Forest Service experience. To meet increasing requirements of the forestry profession Pinchot supported a revision of the curriculum of the State Forest Academy at Mont Alto, an institution supervised by the Department of Forestry. In September 1920 a four-year program of forestry training, with added courses in English and social sciences, replaced a three-year course.[23] The revised curriculum together with the Academy's increasing collegiate program influenced the State Legislature in 1923 to rename the institution as the Pennsylvania State Forest School and helped to win approval of the School's granting of a degree of Bachelor of Science in Forestry.

---

[20] *Forestry Department Report*, 1920–21, p. 15.
[21] *Forestry Department Report*, 1920–21, p. 14.
[22] Memorandum, February 1, 1921, GPP.
[23] Pennsylvania Department of Forests and Waters, *Report, 1922–1924*, p. 14.

While Pinchot continued to stress economic and scientific aspects of forestry, he did not ignore the great value of forests for recreational purposes. In one of his popular Pennsylvania lectures he stated: "The woods are the people's playgrounds and were intended by Nature as such. . . . While the forest is growing lumber it is also furnishing for the people who live in the cities and towns the refuge that attracts when play time comes."[24] He approved funds to open roads and trails that would give greater accessibility to camping sites and other recreational areas in the State Forests and supported the establishment of seven State Forest Parks, nine State Forest Monuments, and two Special Scenic Areas.[25] He envisioned these and other areas not only as wholesome environment for outdoor activity but also as ideal places for study of forest types.

Pinchot's forestry accomplishments in Pennsylvania clearly owed a great deal to favorable legislation. To begin with, his great professional prestige and strategic publicity tactics brought an unprecedented increase in the funds allotted for state forest work. The appropriation voted by the State Legislature for the fiscal period June 1, 1921, to May 31, 1923 ($1,870,000), nearly doubled the biennial amount voted in 1919, before his appointment as Commissioner of Forestry. Moreover, a number of bills strengthening his Department were approved without opposition. Among these were measures to increase the compensation of fire control and other forest personnel, liberalize land acquisition procedures, authorize organizational changes in the Department of Forestry, and bring salaries of the Commissioner of Forestry and his Deputy more in line with those of other principal state officials.[26] Increase of the Commissioner's salary from $5,000 per year to $8,000 in effect provided a higher salary ladder for subordinate forest officers that enhanced the morale and work performance of the entire Department.

---

[24] Pinchot, *Talks on Forestry*, pp. 20–21.
[25] *Forestry Department Report*, 1920–21, p. 18.
[26] *Forestry Department Report*, 1920–21, p. 27.

XVIII

"Forester All the Time"

$\mathbf{P}$INCHOT'S SUCCESS in rallying public support of measures to combat forest fires and in establishing an effective fire protection system was perhaps the greatest of his achievements in advancing the forest work of Pennsylvania. Commenting on the progress made by Pinchot in his publicity campaign against forest fires, the Philadephia *North American* observed: "On no other great public question has there been so rapid and so complete a revolution of public sentiment."[1] Ten years after the institution of Pinchot's statewide fire protection system, R. D. Forbes, Director of the U.S. Allegheny Forest Experiment Station, noted that the system had unquestionably achieved much success in reducing fire losses and thereby had given a great portion of Pennsylvania's forest lands an opportunity "to recuperate naturally from years of former abuse."[2] The system had early proved its worth during the severe forest fire season of 1922 and 1923, when 7,174 forest fires were reported. Next in severity had been the two-year period of 1913–1914 when 2,119 fires were reported. While more than twice as many fires occurred in the 1923–1924 period as had been reported in the earlier severe seasons, the total forest area burned over in the later period was almost 40,000 acres less than in the earlier one.[3]

Moreover, Pinchot's association with forestry in Pennsylvania con-

---

[1] Philadelphia *North American*, September 20, 1920.
[2] Report of Forbes, October 7, 1932, Copeland Report Data, RG 95.
[3] Pennsylvania Department of Forests and Waters, *Report, 1922–1924*, p. 6.

tributed to the progress of the State's forest land acquisition program. Both as a member of the State Forest Commission and later as head of the Department of Forestry a constant objective was to show that the acquisition of forest land by the State was not only a sound financial investment but also a desirable undertaking for protection of the health and general welfare of citizens. His effort aided the movement for expansion of the State forest system. Then, too, private forestry received a boost from his program of assistance to private timberland owners in tree planting and the management of their properties. Under this program Pennsylvania assumed a leading place among the States in encouragement of the reforestation of nonproductive private land and the employment of trained personnel for private forest operations.

On the other hand, in Pinchot's work for Pennsylvania there was a considerable amount of show-window forestry that was emphasized at the expense of silvicultural research and demonstration. While he worked to restore "Penn's Woods," through the organization of large and well-publicized crews of fire fighters assisted by various inspired volunteers and through the purchase of conspicuous idle forest land, he had a tendency to neglect silvicultural operations useful for better management of the "restored" forests. As a member of the Forest Commission he had severely criticized Commissioner Conklin for failure to apply forest principles in a great part of the state forests. Yet as Commissioner himself, he failed to initiate any significant effort to redeem from idleness large forest areas or to institute improvement cuttings over a wide region. His desire to improve his political stature among Pennsylvanians undoubtedly was a factor in causing him to stress those aspects of forest work — notably preventing and fighting forest fires — of greatest popular appeal.

By 1922 Pinchot felt that his stature was sufficiently great to win the governorship of Pennsylvania in the wake of the departed, long-time state political boss, Boies Penrose. Accordingly, he resigned as Commissioner of Forestry on April 13, 1922, to conduct a campaign that was to put him in the state's highest office for the first time and give him national recognition unequaled since the zenith of the conservation crusade. This progression to the political arena brought to an end an historic period of employment in private and public forestry that, with a break after 1910, had spanned thirty years. But it did not terminate Pinchot's deep personal and forcefully demonstrated concern for the advancement of forestry.

During his two terms as governor this concern was manifested in modest but meaningful ways. With his support during the first term

(1923–1927), laws were enacted providing for the prohibition of smoking and building of campfires in or near state forests in time of drought and for the purchase of lands for growing forest tree seedlings. He strongly recommended a proposed constitutional amendment authorizing a bond issue for expansion of the state's forest system and provision for lease of forests for the development of waterpower. Although heavily preoccupied with the unemployment problem during his second term (1931–1935), the Governor succeeded in getting enactment of measures for increased cooperation in fire control with the U.S. Forest Service, construction of essential forest roads, and appointment of local forest advisory councils.

During his service as Commissioner of Forestry and as Governor he led a vigorous campaign for federal government regulation of private forestry. Such regulation was necessary, he maintained, to prevent serious forest devastation long prevalent in the United States, and it would conform with a right exercised in many foreign countries.[4] This type of government regulation was at first rejected by many Americans on constitutional grounds, but continued serious forest devastation on private lands turned many conservationists to Pinchot's view. While opposing any rigid system, the Forest Service in more recent years has persistently advocated "reasonable regulations" based upon national standards to govern forest practices on private lands, which include three-fourths of the commercial forest tracts of the United States. In addition, during the 1920's and 1930's Pinchot mounted strong attacks on presidential and other high-level efforts to transfer control of Forest Service from the Department of Agriculture to the Department of the Interior or a proposed Department of Conservation. Although these attacks were doubtless motivated strongly by prejudices stemming from his earlier "fight for conservation," they were also influenced, according to Henry S. Graves, by his belief that "the federal functions with respect to forests should be coordinated with those of other renewable soil resources in the Department of Agriculture, and that the same principle applies to pasturage and range." Thus, according to this view, he considered management of both forests and range as an "essential feature in stable economic and social development of rural regions."[5]

---

[4] Pinchot to J. Girvin Peters, September 21, 1920, General Correspondence, RG 95; 68th Congress, 1st Sess., Senate Committee on Agriculture and Forestry, *Hearings on S. 1182*, March 28, 1924.

[5] Henry S. Graves, "Early Days with Gifford Pinchot," *Journal of Forestry*, XLIII (August 1945), 552–553.

Probably the most symbolic and touching expression of his interest in forestry — long after his years of employment as a forester — was occasioned by a trip of some 5,000 miles that he took in 1937 at the age of 72. In company with Henry Graves and Herbert Smith, two of his oldest and closest friends in forestry causes, he traveled through national forests in Montana, Idaho, Oregon, and California. Gleefully anticipating being in the woods once again he announced to Graves before his departure: "I am going to get me a tarpaulin in New York tomorrow, and bring a small sleeping bag along with the hope that I can get a few nights in the open anyhow, just for the sake of old times. Gosh it's going to be great!"[6] And so it must have been; for after the trip he exclaimed, "What I saw gave me the greatest satisfaction. The [forest] service is better than it was when I left and everywhere the forests are coming back. What more could a man ask."[7] His abiding interest in forestry was evident four years later when appointment of a new chief of the Forest Service was being considered. He was obviously flattered by suggestions of Congressmen and conservationists that he be appointed temporarily as head of the Service.[8] Raphael Zon, who still maintained close contact with his first chief, found that he was "not averse to take on, at age of 76, temporarily the job of Chief Forester but thought the possibility of such an appointment was very remote" in view of his conflict with Secretary Ickes over the control of the national forests.[9]

In the closing years of his lifelong crusade for forestry, Pinchot concentrated on completing his account of how forestry and conservation came to America, and on the convening of a world conference on natural resources. He had recommended such a conference to various presidents of the United States since 1909. Accepting an award of the National Academy of Sciences on April 19, 1916, he had stated: "Extension of the conservation movement throughout the world may bring the end of all war and lasting peace." Twenty-four years later during World War II he had lamented the fact that war was "still an instrument of national policy for the safeguarding of natural resources or for securing them from other nations." President Franklin D. Roosevelt had supported the world conservation conference proposal shortly before he died in 1945. It was President Truman, however, who sent the

---

[6] Pinchot to H. A. Smith, July 19, 1937, Information and Education Division Correspondence, RG 95.

[7] Pinchot to A. P. Proctor, October 2, 1937, GPP.

[8] Jerry Voorhis to Roosevelt, January 9, 1940, General Correspondence, RG 16.

[9] Official diary of Zon, April 18, 1941, RG 95.

proposal for the conference to the United Nations a few months after Pinchot's death in 1946. As has been noted earlier, the conference was finally held at Lake Success, New York, in August 1949. Here world leaders in conservation expressed the view so long held by Pinchot that international cooperation in the conservation and use of natural resources might well remove one of the most formidable obstacles to permanent peace. Cooperation in this direction has become one of the most important economic and scientific objectives of the United Nations.

Pinchot's other significant undertaking for the forestry cause in his last years was the completion of *Breaking New Ground,* his autobiographical work dedicated, as might be expected, to the "men and women of the Forest Service." As early as 1912 he had begun to collect material for this personal story of American forestry and the conservation movement.[10] Political and other public activities of his middle years and declining health of his last years tended to prevent concentrated attention to this task. But with the help of Herbert Smith and other long-time associates the work was substantially finished in 1945 and it was published posthumously in 1947. It dealt with major phases of his forestry career from 1892 to 1910 and defended his actions in leading forest and conservation disputes of the period. Despite its considerable bias, foresters and historians agree that it is an invaluable account of an eyewitness to crucial struggles and victories in the early history of American forestry.

Forester still of mind and might, Pinchot died October 4, 1946, at the age of eight-one. A few months earlier, speaking on the occasion of the fortieth anniversary of the Forest Service's establishment he had said: "I have been a Governor every now and then, but I am a forester all the time — have been, and shall be, to my dying day." In a sense this declaration rang remarkably true. Within a few days of his death he was working on a revised forest management plan for his estate at Milford, Pennsylvania.[11]

Progress toward sound forestry practice on both private and public timberlands of the United States is the chief monument to the life of Gifford Pinchot. In North Carolina and New York he provided the nation with the first examples of successful scientific forestry to show an increasing number of private forest owners the practicality and profit-

---

[10] Pinchot to G. G. Anderson, April 19, 1912, Operations Division Correspondence, RG 95.

[11] Press release of the U.S. Forest Service, October 10, 1946, RG 95.

ability of managing forests for continuous timber crops. His dynamic leadership gave the first great impetus to acceptance of the principle of developing all resources on forest lands for the "greatest good to the greatest number." This involved the adjustment of one forest use to another so that the net public benefit would result — to obtain the greatest total of crops, uses, and services. Thus there evolved the multiple-use policy which now guides the administration of national forests and a growing number of state forests.

Finally, Pinchot brought to the forestry movement a great talent for publicity. He came on the national scene at an opportune time. Events at the turn of the century had blazed the way for the concept of forest protection, and much discussion about forest destruction had been aroused. Still the idea of conservative use of forests had to be nurtured into a fact. Dramatization and education were essential. Interests hostile because of ignorance and selfishness had to be reconciled, regulated, or educated. It was a task that called for great devotion to public service and great ability to mold and guide public opinion in the face of powerful assault. Pinchot performed this task with remarkable success. On national and state levels his mission was to convince Americans that they had a great possession that was rapidly dwindling away, and he awakened them to the vital importance of preserving this possession. In doing this he helped to make the conservation of forests and related natural resources one of the most crucial issues of the twentieth century.

Bibliography

EXPLANATORY STATEMENT
ON PRIMARY SOURCES

Records of the Forest Service in the National Archives, Washington, D.C., have been by far the most useful and informative primary documentary source in the writing of this book. These records cover all phases of Gifford Pinchot's administration of the Forest Service and include considerable data concerning his conservation and nonfederal activities. Especially useful were the following series among this archival record group: general correspondence of the Chief's Office, and various records of the Division of Operations, Office of Information and Education, and Research Division.

Personal papers of Pinchot transferred to the Manuscripts Division of the Library of Congress, Washington, D.C., constituted another important documentary source for this study. A substantial body of these papers has been grouped under the subject headings "forestry" and "conservation." Many other pertinent papers were found in general correspondence files arranged alphabetically by name of the correspondent. In general, this collection was very useful in furnishing data concerning Pinchot's work as a private forester and as Commissioner of Forestry for Pennsylvania. Extant fragmentary records of the Pennsylvania Department of Forestry do not appear to supplement in any major degree the data on Pinchot's work in Pennsylvania found in these papers.

Useful also in many respects were other records in the National Archives such as the "General Records" of the Department of Agriculture, and "General Records" of the Department of the Interior. Since the records of the Forest Service and the personal papers of Pinchot seemed to be so complete with letters received and copies of letters sent, it did not seem necessary to examine extensively the records of some government agencies and the personal papers of various individuals with whom Pinchot corresponded and worked as a forester. However, citations in the study show that these other sources were not ignored.

Pinchot's autobiographical work *Breaking New Ground* yielded many facts concerning his early career which were not readily available in archival and manuscript collections. It also served as a useful summary of some of his principal views. For controversial aspects of forestry and conservation the book was naturally very pro-Pinchot and could be used only to obtain that point of view. His *Fight for Conservation* also provided in summary form some of the basic concepts of his mission. Published articles and speeches by Pinchot also supplemented unpublished data relating to his thought and served to illustrate the prolificness with which he wrote and spoke for forestry and conservation.

ABBREVIATIONS FREQUENTLY USED

GPP   Gifford Pinchot Papers
RG   Record Group

Record Groups in the National Archives, Washington, D.C., are, in the footnotes to the text, cited in the first instance with their numbers and titles, and thereafter with their numbers only. The bibliography gives a complete list of the Record Groups cited or examined.

BIBLIOGRAPHIC AIDS

Library of Congress, *Select List of References on the Conservation of Natural Resources in the United States.* Washington: Government Printing Office, 1912. 110 pp. Also supplementary lists, 1934, 1938, 1942.

National Archives, *Preliminary Inventory of the Records of the Forest Service.* Compiled by Harold T. Pinkett. Washington, 1949. 17 pp.

———, *Preliminary Report upon Records Relating to the Ballinger-Pinchot Controversy.* Prepared by T. R. Schellenberg. Washington, 1940 (MS). 9 pp.

U.S. Department of Agriculture, *Index to Publications of the U.S. Department of Agriculture, 1901–1925.* Washington: Government Printing Office, 1932. 2689 pp.

———, *Bibliography on Soil Erosion and Soil and Water Conservation.* Washington: Government Printing Office, 1938. 651 pp.

———, Library, *A Guide for Courses in the History of American Agriculture.* Compiled by E. E. Edwards. Washington, 1939. 192 pp.

PRIMARY SOURCES

NATIONAL ARCHIVES, WASHINGTON, D.C.
Record Group No. 16, General Records of the Department of Agriculture.
Record Group No. 46, Records of the United States Senate.
Record Group No. 48, General Records of the Department of the Interior.
Record Group No. 49, Records of the General Land Office.
Record Group No. 57, Records of the Geological Survey.
Record Group No. 95, Records of the Forest Service.
Record Group No. 114, Records of the Soil Conservation Service.
Record Group No. 155, Records of the Bureau of Reclamation.

MANUSCRIPTS IN THE LIBRARY OF CONGRESS, WASHINGTON, D.C.
Gifford Pinchot Papers
Theodore Roosevelt Papers

UNITED STATES GOVERNMENT PUBLICATIONS
All entries in this series were published by the Government Printing Office, Washington, D.C., unless otherwise specified.
55th Congress, 1st Session, Senate Document No. 105, *Report of the Committee of the National Academy of Science.* 1897. 47 pp.
————, 2d Session, Senate Document, No. 189, *Report on the Examination of the Forest Reserves.* 1898. 118 pp.
56th Congress, Committee on the Public Lands, House of Representatives, *Hearings on the Reclamation and Disposal of the Arid Public Lands of the West.* 1901. 135 pp.
57th Congress, 1st Session, Senate Document No. 84, *Report of the Secretary of Agriculture in Relation to the Forests, Rivers and Mountains of the Southern Appalachian Region.* 1902. 210 pp.
58th Congress, 3d Session, Senate Document No. 189, *Report of the Public Lands Commission.* 1905. 373 pp.
59th Congress, 2d Session, House Report No. 8147, *Report of the Committee on Expenditures in the Department of Agriculture.* 1907.
60th Congress, 1st Session, Senate Document No. 91, *Report of the Secretary of Agriculture on the Southern Appalachian and White Mountain Watersheds.* 1908. 39 pp.
————, 1st Session, Senate Document No. 325, *Preliminary Report of the Inland Waterways Commission.* 1907. 701 pp.
————, 1st Session, Senate Document No. 485, *Attendance of Members of the Forest Service at Meetings and Conventions, 1907.*
————, 2d Session, House Document No. 1425, *Proceedings of a Conference of Governors.* 1908. 451 pp.
————, 2d Session, Senate Document No. 676, *Report of the National Conservation Commission.* 1909. 3 vols. 276, 771, 793 pp.

61st Congress, 3d Session, Senate Document No. 719, *Investigation of the Interior Department and the Bureau of Forestry.* 1911. 13 vols.

68th Congress, 1st Session, Senate Committee on Agriculture and Forestry, *Hearings on S. 1182,* March 28, 1924.

73d Congress, 1st Session, Senate Document No. 12, *A National Plan for American Forestry* (Smith, Tillotson, and O'Donnell). 1933. 2 vols.

81st Congress, 2d Session, House Print, House Committee on Agriculture, *Research and Related Services in the U.S. Department of Agriculture.* 1953. 3 vols.

House of Representatives, Committee on Agriculture, *A Report on the Influence of Forests on Climate and Floods* (by W. L. Moore). 1910. 38 pp.

U.S. Department of Agriculture, Division of Forestry Bulletin 24, pt. 1, *A Primer of Forestry* (by Gifford Pinchot). 1903. 88 pp.; pt. 2 *Practical Forestry.* 1905. 288 pp.

————, Forest Service, *The Use Book. Regulations and Instructions for the Use of the National Forest Reserves* (by Gifford Pinchot). 1906. 208 pp.

————, Forest Service. *The Conservation of Natural Resources* (by Gifford Pinchot). 1908. 12 pp.

————, Forest Service, Circular No. 21, *Practical Assistance to Farmers, Lumbermen, and Others in Handling Forest Lands.* 1898. 8 pp.

————, Forest Service, Circular No. 35, *Forest Preservation and National Prosperity.* 1905. 31 pp.

————, *Forest Plantation at Biltmore, North Carolina* (by Ferdinand W. Haasis). Miscellaneous Publications No. 61. 1930. 30 pp.

————, Forest Service, *The Response of Government to Agriculture* (by Arthur P. Chew). 1937. 108 pp.

————, Forest Service, *Early American Soil Conservationists* (by Angus McDonald). 1941. 63 pp.

U.S. Department of the Interior, Office of the Secretary, *Not Guilty. An Official Inquiry into the Charges Made by Glavis and Pinchot Against Richard A. Ballinger, Secretary of the Interior, 1909–1911* (by Harold L. Ickes). 1940. 58 pp.

————, Conservation Bulletin 39, *A Century of Conservation.* 1950. 36 pp.

U.S. Philippine Commission, *Fourth Annual Report,* pt. 2. 1904.

OTHER U.S. GOVERNMENT PUBLICATIONS,
MAINLY FOR THE PERIOD 1890–1910:

Congressional Record

Annual Reports of the following officials:

Secretary of Agriculture

Secretary of the Interior

Chief of the Forest Service, and Reports of the Forester

Chief of the Geological Survey

Commissioner of the General Land Office

Department of Agriculture Yearbooks
Messages and Papers of the Presidents (edited by James D. Richardson).
New York. Vols. 14–16.

NEW JERSEY STATE GOVERNMENT PUBLICATIONS:
Geological Survey of *New Jersey, Annual Report of the State Geologist,
1895.* Trenton, 1896. 200 pp.
Geological Survey of *New Jersey, Annual Report of the State Geologist,
1898.* Trenton, 1899. 210 pp.

NORTH CAROLINA STATE GOVERNMENT PUBLICATIONS:
Geological Survey of North Carolina, *Timber, Trees and Forests of North
Carolina* (by Gifford Pinchot, with William W. Ashe). Bulletin No. 6,
Raleigh, 1897. 227 pp.

PENNSYLVANIA STATE GOVERNMENT PUBLICATIONS:
Report of the Department of Forestry, 1918–1919. Harrisburg, 1920. 26
pp.
Report of the Department of Forestry, 1920–1921. Harrisburg, 1922.
49 pp.
*Report of the Department of Forests and Waters, January 1, 1922 to
May 31, 1924.* Harrisburg, 1924. 26 pp.
Talks on Forestry by Gifford Pinchot (Pennsylvania Department of For-
estry Bulletin 32). Harrisburg, 1923. 28 pp.

UNITED NATIONS PUBLICATIONS:
Department of Economic Affairs, *Proceedings of the United Nations,
Scientific Conference on the Conservation and Utilization of Resources,
17 August — 6 September 1949. Lake Success, N.Y.* Volume 1. *Plenary
Meetings.* New York, 1950. 431 pp.

NON-GOVERNMENT DOCUMENTARY COMPILATIONS:
Bancroft, Frederic (ed.), *Speeches, Correspondence and Political Papers
of Carl Schurz.* New York: G. P. Putnam's Sons, 1913. 6 vols.
Morison, Elting E. (ed.), *The Letters of Theodore Roosevelt.* Cambridge,
Mass.: Harvard University Press, 1951. 2 vols. 1549 pp.
Taft, William H., *Presidential Addresses and State Papers.* New York:
Doubleday, Page and Co., 1910. 612 pp.

BOOKS (NON-GOVERNMENT) BY GIFFORD PINCHOT:
The Adirondack Spruce. New York: Critic Co., 1898. 150 pp.
Biltmore Forest: Account of First Year's Work. Chicago: R. R. Donnelley
and Sons, 1893. 49 pp.
Breaking New Ground. New York: Harcourt, Brace and Co., 1947. 522 pp.
The Fight for Conservation. New York: Doubleday, Page and Co., 1910.
152 pp.

The White Pine (with Henry S. Graves). New York: Century Co., 1896. 102 pp.

ARTICLES AND PUBLISHED SPEECHES BY GIFFORD PINCHOT:

"How Conservation Began in the United States," *Agriculture History,* XI, 255–265 (October 1937).

"Forestry on Private Lands," *Annals of the American Academy of Political and Social Science,* XXXIII (3), 3–12 (1909).

"Government Forestry Abroad," *Publications of the American Economic Association,* VI, 191–238 (May 1891).

"How the National Forests Were Won," *American Forests and Forest Life,* XXXVI, 615–619, 674 (1930).

"Turning Point of National Prosperity," *American Industries,* VII (8), 14–15 (1908).

"The Proposed Eastern Forest Reserves," *Appalachia,* XI (2), 134–143 (1906).

"Progress in Forest Reservation," *Century Magazine* (June 1904).

"Home Building for the Nation," *Conservation,* XV (9), 521–522 (1909).

"Profession of Forestry," *Forester,* V, 155–160 (1899).

"In the Philippine Forests," *Forestry and Irrigation,* IX, 66–72 (February 1903).

"Forestry on the Farm," *Forestry and Irrigation,* IX, 432–435 (September 1903).

"Improvement of Our Heritage," *Forestry and Irrigation,* XIV, 148–152 (March 1908).

"Roosevelt's Part in Forestry," *Journal of Forestry,* XVII, 122–124 (1914).

"The Public Good Comes First," *Journal of Forestry,* XXXIX, 208–212 (February 1941).

"Relation of Forests and Fires," *National Geographic Magazine,* X, 393–403 (October 1899).

"Forestry Abroad and at Home," *National Geographic Magazine,* XVI, 351–360 (August 1905).

"Forest Situation in New England," *New England Magazine,* XXXIX, 404–405 (December 1908).

"The A. B. C. of Conservation," *Outlook,* XCIII (14), 770–772 (1909).

"Chief Forester Visits Colorado," *Southern Lumberman,* LIX (704), 29–30 (March 20, 1909).

"Trees and Civilization," *World's Work,* II, 986–995 (July 1901).

SECONDARY SOURCES

BOOKS

Bailey, I. W., and H. A. Spoehr, *The Role of Research in the Development of Forestry in America.* New York, 1929. 250 pp.

Cameron, Jenks, *The Development of Government Forest Control in the United States.* (Institute for Government Research.) Baltimore: The Johns Hopkins Press, 1928. 471 pp.

Chittenden, L. E., *Personal Reminiscences, 1840–1890.* New York: Richmond, Croscup & Co. 1893. 434 pp.

Fausold, Martin L., *Gifford Pinchot, Bull Moose Progressive.* Syracuse: Syracuse University Press, 1961. 275 pp.

Greeley, William B., *Forests and Men.* New York: Doubleday and Company, Inc., 1951.

Gulick, Luther H., *American Forest Policy, A Study of Government Administrative and Economic Control.* New York: Duell, Sloan and Pearce, 1951. 275 pp.

Harding, T. Swann, *Two Blades of Grass, A History of Scientific Development in the United States Department of Agriculture.* Norman: University of Oklahoma Press, 1947. 352 pp.

Hart, Albert B., and Herbert R. Ferleger (eds.), *Theodore Roosevelt Cyclopedia.* New York: Roosevelt Memorial Association, 1951. 674 pp.

Hays, Samuel, *Conservation and the Gospel of Efficiency.* Cambridge: Harvard University Press, 1959. 297 pp.

Hibbard, B. H., *History of the Public Land Policies.* Madison: University of Wisconsin Press, 1965. 591 pp.

Irving, Washington, *A Tour of the Prairies.* New York: John W. Lovell Co., 1833. 153 pp.

Ise, John, *The United States Forest Policy.* New Haven: Yale University Press, 1924. 395 pp.

————, *The United States Oil Policy.* New Haven: Yale University Press, 1926. 547 pp.

Kinney, J. P., *The Development of Forest Law in America.* New York: John Wiley and Sons, Inc., 1917. 252 pp.

Lord, Russell, *Behold Our Land.* Boston: Houghton Mifflin Co., 1938. 310 pp.

McGeary, M. Nelson, *Gifford Pinchot, Forester-Politician.* Princeton: Princeton University Press, 1960. 481 pp.

Marsh, G. P., *Man and Nature.* New York: Scribner, Armstrong, & Co., 1864. (Retitled *The Earth as Modified by Human Action.* 1874).

Mason, Alpheus T., *Bureaucracy Convicts Itself. The Ballinger-Pinchot Controversy of 1910.* New York: Viking Press, 1941.

Mowry, George E., *Theodore Roosevelt and the Progressive Movement.* Madison: University of Wisconsin Press, 1946. 405 pp.

Paxon, Frederic L., *History of the American Frontier.* New York: Houghton Mifflin Co., 1925. 598 pp.

Peffer, E. Louise, *The Closing of the Public Domain, Disposal and Reservation Policies, 1900–50.* Stanford: Stanford University Press, 1951. 372 pp.

Pringle, Henry F., *The Life and Times of William Howard Taft.* New York and Toronto: Farrar and Rinehart, Inc., 1939. 2 vols. 1106, 241 pp.

Quick, Herbert, *American Inland Waterways.* New York: G. P. Putnam's Sons, 1909. 241 pp.

Richardson, Elmo R., *The Politics of Conservation, Crusades and Controversies, 1897–1913.* Berkeley: University of California Press, 1962. 305 pp.

Robbins, Roy M., *Our Landed Heritage, The Public Domain, 1776–1936.* Princeton: Princeton University Press, 1942. 450 pp.

Rodgers, Andrew D., III, *Bernhard Eduard Fernow.* Princeton: Princeton University Press, 1959. 623 pp.

Roosevelt, Theodore, *Autobiography.* New York: Charles Scribner's Sons, 1929. 597 pp.

Schenck, Carl A., *The Biltmore Story.* St. Paul: American Forest History Foundation, 1955. 224 pp.

Smith, Darrell H., *The Forest Service, Its History, Activities, and Organization.* (Institute for Government Research.) Baltimore: The Johns Hopkins Press, 1930. 268 pp.

Stahl, Rose M., *The Ballinger-Pinchot Controversy.* (Smith College Studies in History, XI, No. 2.) Northampton, 1926. 138 pp.

Stimson, Henry L., and McGeorge Bundy, *On Active Service in Peace and War.* New York: Harper and Brothers, 1948. 698 pp.

Turner, F. J., *The Frontier in American History.* New York: H. Holt & Co., 1920.

Van Hise, Charles, and Loomis Havemeyer, *Conservation of Our Natural Resources.* New York: Macmillan Co., 1936. 551 pp.

Winters, R. K. (ed.), *Fifty Years of Forestry in the United States.* Washington: Society of American Foresters, 1950. 385 pp.

ARTICLES

Anonymous, "Patriotism That Counts," *Century Magazine,* LXXV, 474–476 (July 1908).

———, "Pinchot-Ballinger Controversy," *Outlook,* XCIII, 131–133 (September 23, 1909).

———, "Pinchot vs. Ballinger," *Nation,* LXXXIX, 270 (September 23, 1909).

———, "Gifford Pinchot–Eighty Years Young," *Journal of Forestry,* XLIII, 547–548 (August 1945).

———, "White House Conference on Natural Resources," *American Review of Reviews,* XXXVII, 642–644 (June 1908).

Baker, Charles W., "The Necessity for State or Federal Regulation of Water Power Development," *Annals of the American Academy of Political and Social Science,* XXXIII, 583–596 (May 1909).

Barnes, Will C., "Gifford Pinchot, Forester," *McClure's Magazine,* XXXI, 319–327 (July 1908).

Bates, J. Leonard, "Fulfilling American Democracy: The Conservation Movement, 1907 to 1921," *Mississippi Valley Historical Review,* XLIV (June 1957).

Chautauquan (Special Conservation Number), LV (June 1909).

Coffman, John D., "Forestry in the Department of the Interior," *Journal of Forestry*, XXXIX, 84–91 (February 1941).

Ganoe, John T., "Some Constitutional and Political Aspects of the Ballinger-Pinchot Controversy," *Pacific Historical Review*, III, 323–333 (September 1934).

Glavis, L. R., "The Whitewashing of Ballinger — Are the Guggenheims in Charge of the Department of Interior?" *Collier's Weekly*, XLIV, 15–17 (November 13, 1909).

Graves, Henry S., "Early Days with Gifford Pinchot," *Journal of Forestry*, XLIII, 550–553 (August 1945).

Gray, L. C., "The Economic Possibilities of Conservation," *Quarterly Journal of Economics*, XXVII, 497–519 (May 1913).

Hall, William L., "Hail to the Chief," *Journal of Forestry*, XLIII, 553–557 (August 1945).

Holmes, Joseph A., "A Rational Basis for the Conservation of Mineral Resources," *Transactions of the American Institute of Mining Engineers* (February 1909).

Hosmer, Ralph S., "Some Recollections of Gifford Pinchot, 1898–1904," *Journal of Forestry*, XLIII, 558–562 (August 1945).

————, "The Society of American Foresters, An Historical Summary," *Journal of Forestry*, XLVIII, 756–777 (November 1950).

Hough, Emerson, "The Wasteful West," *Saturday Evening Post*, CLXXVIII, 6–8, 23–24 (December 23, 1905).

Johnson, Emory R., "Conservation of Natural Resources," *Annals of the American Academy of Political and Social Science*, XXXIII, 487, 751 (May 1909).

McGee, W J, "The Five-Fold Functions of Government," *Popular Science* (September 1910), pp. 274–285.

————, "The Cult of Conservation," *Conservation* (September 1908), pp. 469–472.

Martin, John, "Significance of the White House Conference," *Charities and the Commons*, XX, 471–473 (July 1908).

Matthews, J. R., "Ballinger-Pinchot Controversy," *Hampton's Magazine*, XXII, 659 (November 1909).

Nelson, Charles A., "The Forest Products Laboratory," *Forest History*, XI, 6–14, (July 1967).

Pack, Charles L., "Gifford Pinchot," *American Review of Reviews*, LXXI, 598–600 (June 1925).

Page, Walter H., "Gifford Pinchot, Awakener of the Nation," *World's Work*, XIX, 12662–12668 (March 1910).

Palmer, Frederick L., "Pinchot's Fight for the Trees," *Collier's Weekly*, XL (No. 10), 13–14 (November 30, 1907).

Penick, James L., Jr., "The Age of the Bureaucrat, Another View of the Ballinger-Pinchot Controversy," *Forest History*, VII, 15–21 (Spring–Summer 1963).

Pinchot, Cornelia B., "Gifford Pinchot and the Conservation Ideal," *Journal of Forestry*, XLVIII, 83–86 (February 1950).

Pinkett, Harold T., "Records of Research Units of the United States Forest Service in the National Archives," *Journal of Forestry*, XLV, 272–275 (April 1947).

———, "Gifford Pinchot at Biltmore," *North Carolina Historical Review*, XXXIV, 346–357 (July 1957).

———, "Gifford Pinchot, Consulting Forester, 1893–1898," *New York History*, XXXIX, 34–49 (January 1958).

Price, Overton W., "George W. Vanderbilt, Pioneer in Forestry," *American Forestry*, XX, 422 (June 1914).

Rakestraw, Laurence, "Forest Missionary, George Patrick Ahern, 1894–1899," *Montana*, IX, 36–44 (October 1959).

Schmitz, Henry, "To Whom the Nation Owes Most," *Journal of Forestry*, XLIII, 563–565 (August 1945).

Shantz, H. L., "Economic Aspects of Conservation," *Journal of Forestry*, XXXIX, 741–747 (September 1941).

Smith, Herbert A., "The Early Forestry Movement in the United States," *Agricultural History*, XII, 326–346 (October 1938).

Titsworth, Frederick S., "Notes on the Legal Aspects of the Conservation Problem," *Proceedings of the Colorado Scientific Society*, IX, 315–334 (February 5, 1910).

Tryon, F. G., "Conservation," *Encyclopedia of the Social Sciences*, IV, 227–229 (1931).

Turner, Frederick J., "Social Forces in American History," *American Historical Review*, XVI, 217–233 (January 1911).

Wehrwein, George S., "Conservation," *Journal of Land and Public Utility Economics*, XII, 421–422 (November 1936).

Wirt, George H., "Joseph Trimble Rothrock, Father of Forestry in Pennsylvania," *American-German Review*, VIII, 5–8 (February 1942).

Zon, Raphael, "Public Good Comes First," *American Forests*, LIII, 544–547 (November 1946).

NEWSPAPERS CITED

Boston (Massachusetts) *Transcript*
Churchman
Cincinnati (Ohio) *Commercial*
Cincinnati (Ohio) *Enquirer*
Concord (New Hampshire) *Monitor*
Denver (Colorado) *News*
Denver (Colorado) *Republican*
(Denver, Colorado) *Rocky Mountain News*
Grand Rapids (Michigan) *News*

Philadelphia (Pennsylvania) *North American*
Philadelphia (Pennsylvania) *Public Ledger*
Providence (Rhode Island) *Journal*
Pueblo (Colorado) *Star Journal*
San Francisco (California) *Bulletin*
Spokane (Washington) *Chronicle*
Spokane (Washington) *Spokesman-Review*
Washington, D.C. *National Tribune*
Washington, D.C. *Post*
Wheeling (West Virginia) *News*

Index

A Note on the Author

Harold T. Pinkett is editor of the *American Archivist* and deputy director of the Records Appraisal Division of the National Archives. Born in Salisbury, Maryland, he received his A.B. from Morgan College, his A.M. from the University of Pennsylvania, and his Ph.D. from American University. Mr. Pinkett headed the former Agricultural Branch of the National Archives, and has been a Fellow of the Society of American Archivists since 1962. His first book, *Gifford Pinchot: Private and Public Forester*, is the 1968 award winner of the Agricultural History Society. University of Illinois Press